Reach and Teach

Reach and Teach

Educational Short-Term Missions
as a Ministry of the Local Church

Steve Curtis

Foreword by
Flip Buys

WIPF & STOCK · Eugene, Oregon

REACH AND TEACH
Educational Short-Term Missions as a Ministry of the Local Church

Copyright © 2016 Steve Curtis. All rights reserved. Except for brief quotations in critical publications or reviews, no part of this book may be reproduced in any manner without prior written permission from the publisher. Write: Permissions, Wipf and Stock Publishers, 199 W. 8th Ave., Suite 3, Eugene, OR 97401.

Wipf & Stock
An Imprint of Wipf and Stock Publishers
199 W. 8th Ave., Suite 3
Eugene, OR 97401

www.wipfandstock.com

PAPERBACK ISBN: 978-1-4982-9622-9
HARDCOVER ISBN: 978-1-4982-9624-3
EBOOK ISBN: 978-1-4982-9623-6

Manufactured in the U.S.A.

All Scripture quotations taken from *The Holy Bible, English Standard Version*® (ESV®)

Copyright © 2001 by Crossway, a publishing ministry of Good News Publishers. All rights reserved.

To Rissa, for your love through our years together, for faithfully walking with me through the valleys and upon the peaks, for bringing a joy to my life I had never known, and for truly being my excellent wife . . . far more precious than jewels (Prov 31:10);

To Mom and Dad, who modeled the love of Christ before my eyes and taught me diligently the things of God, talking of them when you sit in your house, and when you walk by the way, and when you lie down, and when you rise (Deut 6:7);

To all my family, our friends from Myrtle Grove Evangelical Presbyterian Church, and the board members of Timothy Two Project, International, for your love, your friendship, your honesty, and your wise counsel, which all served to "sharpen" me, as you affirmed our call to the mission field and sent us to do that work God has called us to do (Prov 27:5, 9, 17);

To the pastors and church leaders throughout the world whom God has called me to serve and who humble and amaze me with their passionate desire and diligent commitment to grow in the grace and knowledge of our Lord (2 Pet 3:18); and

Above all, to the One who loved me and gave Himself for me that I might have peace with God (Eph 5:2; Rom 5:1): my blessed Redeemer, Christ Jesus the Lord, who lives and reigns from everlasting to everlasting . . .

Thank you.

Soli Deo Gloria

Contents

List of Figures | viii
Author's Note | ix
Foreword by Flip Buys | xi
Abbreviations | xiii

1 Introduction | 1
2 The Roots of the American Missions Tradition | 12
3 The Cry of the Global Church and the American Response | 30
4 Developing an EdSTM Ministry in the Local Church | 49
5 Conclusion | 88

Glossary | 95
Appendix A: Church Survey Questions and Results | 97
Appendix B: Missions Agency Survey Questions and Results | 101
Appendix C: Pastor's Interview Questions and Responses | 105
Bibliography | 119

Figures

Figure 1: The Rise of Non-Western Missionaries | 33

Figure 2: Distribution of Full-Time Missionaries | 34

Figure 3: Distribution of Missions Workers by Time | 36

Figure 4: Distribution of Missions Workers by Task | 37

Figure 5: Changes in Mission Foci (2001-2008) | 39

Figure 6: Agency-Based STM by Task | 41

Figure 7: Church-Based STM by Task | 42

Figure 8: EdSTM Model | 49

Author's Note

There are some qualifications to the research in this book. First, it considers missions from a Protestant perspective; therefore, missions activities of the Roman Catholic Church will only be addressed for historical context. Further, this study is concerned with missions from an evangelical perspective; therefore, the work of non-evangelical or "mainline" Protestant denominations will not be considered.[1] Also, the research for this paper is restricted to missions activities within the United States: specifically, the work of U.S.-based missions organizations and local churches in the United States. Finally, I do not claim to make universal statements vis-à-vis educational missions, as there are missionaries, not officially connected to or endorsed by missions agencies or, in some cases, even by the local church. Ascertaining hard data on all such missionaries would be impossible. Therefore, the data contained herein, and the proposal resulting from an analysis of that data, is based solely upon the quantifiable information obtainable through surveys, interviews, and published sources.

1. For a brief yet helpful distinction between "mainline" and "evangelical" missions, see Moreau et al, *Introducing World Missions*, 142–143.

Foreword

New ways of becoming part
of the answer to Jesus' prayer

> *"The harvest is plentiful, but the labourers are few; therefore pray earnestly to the Lord of the harvest to send out labourers into his harvest." (Mt 9:37–38).*

There are still millions of Christian pastors in the developing world who are preaching on pulpits and planting churches without having had any theological education or having received very limited theological education. The call of Jesus to pray for harvesters to be sent out is still just as relevant as it was when He spoke it to the apostles.

To send out full time, well trained missionaries from a developed country to go and do evangelism and plant churches in less developed countries among unreached, or partly reached, people groups is very good, but it is like picking apples. Another way is to plant apple trees! That is done by training indigenous leaders to become better equipped to fulfil their calling to be shepherds of God's flock among their own people. If they can be helped to become trainers themselves, real multiplication will take place.

If we have a passion for the wellbeing of the church of Christ in our hearts, we will do everything in our power to support indigenous pastors to become well trained.

It is very encouraging to hear and see many churches in the developed world sending out church members on short term mission outreaches. Unfortunately, these short term outreaches mostly focus on physical activities like erecting church buildings or doing some manual work. There have also been incidents where short

Foreword

term missionaries were not well prepared and did their outreach in such a way that they have hurt the poor and did more damage than really helping indigenous Christians. Sometimes short term outreaches just become glorified tourism and sightseeing endeavours and no real mission work is done.

This raises the burning question: How do you assist untrained pastors in remote areas to be trained and equipped in such a way that they are able to integrate solid biblical teaching in their minds and hearts? How do you enrich their lives and ministries so that they may gain an experiential knowledge of sound evangelical theology that will really address problems and challenges they encounter in their own context? How do you help them to develop indigenous lecturers to train their own pastors? How can short term missionaries be equipped and trained to gain such a clear grip of God's transforming grace in their own lives that they can convey it to poorly trained indigenous pastors in the developing world to be channels of his grace where God open doors for them to serve?

The use of short term missionaries to contribute to the training of pastors who have had no or very limited training is largely still an untapped force in God's kingdom.

Steve Curtis has gained years of experience to be a "mobile missionary instructor" in the most remote places among unreached people groups in developing counties. He has developed study guides and manuals that stimulate indigenous pastors to integrate the content in their own lives and contextualize it for the most effective use among their own people.

In this book he deals with all aspects of the training and thrusting out of church members as short term educators in God's worldwide harvest field.

My prayer is that this book will be used to raise up a significant force of short term missionary educators to multiply the number of labourers in God's worldwide harvest.

Dr Flip Buys

Experienced missionary, cross cultural theological educator,
and International Director of World Reformed Fellowship

Abbreviations

AD	Adult Discipleship
CES	Chinese Evangelization Society
CIM	China Inland Mission
EdSTM	Educational Short-Term Missions
EdSTMer	Educational Short-Term Missionary
LTM	Long-Term Missions
LTMer	Long-Term Missionary
OM	Operation Mobilization
TTPI	Timothy Two Project, International
STM	Short-Term Missions
STMer	Short-Term Missionary
SVM	Student Volunteer Movement
WEC	Worldwide Evangelization for Christ
YWAM	Youth with a Mission

1

Introduction

On a typical, tropical day in the Philippines, I found myself in a most atypical circumstance: hunkered down in the back of a van with darkly-tinted windows, bouncing up a dirt road in the mountainous regions of Mindanao. I was on my way to teach a group of pastors in an area known for Muslim militants who had a history of kidnapping Westerners—especially Western missionaries. After about two hours, we arrived at a ramshackle building and I was hustled inside. Introductions were made all around, and I was intrigued to meet the pastors with whom I would be working. One—I'll call him Peter—had a particularly interesting story to tell. He related how a Western missionary had come through Manila some years ago, where Peter (not yet converted) happened to hear the gospel for the first time, through an interpreter at an evangelistic crusade. He received gladly the message of Christ's vicarious work and was the first convert at the crusade. Over the following days, others were converted, until there was a small group of new believers. Peter, as the first and perhaps the most enthusiastic convert, began to urge the missionary to teach him more about this Savior, the Son of God. The missionary responded by sharing Bible stories with Peter during the day before each night's worship service. He also responded publicly in one service, with a magnanimous presentation of a beautiful, gilded Bible as a gift for Peter. Though the Bible was in English (a language foreign to Peter at the time), his zeal did not flag; in fact, he began to ask if he could study or apprentice with the missionary. To his dismay, he learned that the missionary's time in the Philippines was nearing its end. He was assured that all hope was not lost, however, as the missionary pointed around to the little crowd that constituted a new Philippine *church*. Placing his hands on Peter's shoulders, the missionary looked him in the eye and gave him the solemn charge that would change Peter's life: *You will be their pastor.*

Thankfully, Peter's story ends well, as he was able soon after this encounter to travel to a distant city to attend Bible school before returning to take up the mantle as pastor; first in Manila and, later, in Mindanao where he related this story. His point, however, was unmistakable: there are many pastors in the developing world who are ill-equipped to shepherd a congregation and who, in many cases, are only the pastor by virtue of the fact that some evangelist or missionary—believing his Great Commission work to be done with the simple presentation of the gospel—left a vacuum in his wake that had to be filled. As a missionary to several such people groups, I have personally witnessed the effects of this lack of preparation in churches throughout the Majority World.[1] It is, of course, a wonderful thing when the gospel is presented in the farthest corners of the globe, and men and women turn to Christ. However, the Great Commission work does not end there; the command includes the specific charge to "make disciples of all nations . . . teaching them to observe all that I have commanded . . ." (Matt 28:19–20).

Thus, the Great Commission is not wholly fulfilled when churches simply send out teams to engage in relief efforts or development projects. Still, many American churches have convinced themselves that their work stops there. After reading the manuscript for this book, one former pastor confided that he was convicted by the all-too-common anemic response of the local church to the real work of missions. Another noted how, after going on a short-term missions trip and building a church, he was similarly

---

1. Tennent uses the term *Majority World* "to refer collectively to all the Christians who inhabit Asia, Africa, and Latin America" (*Invitation*, 17). This is how I use the term in this book, as well. A fuller discussion may be found in the Glossary.

Introduction

convicted when the team left the country behind with a new building but with no meaningfully equipped leadership.

There is a critical need for the Great Commission mandate of *teaching* in the churches of the Majority World; more particularly, there is a need to teach those who will be teaching the churches—the *pastors*. One solution is to deploy qualified teachers on short-term educational missions, and one often overlooked resource for such teachers is the cadre of lay ministers in the American church. The model I present here considers this solution.

The Heart of the Problem

At present in many quarters of the world, formal theological training is out of the reach of many pastors and would-be pastors. Sometimes the impediment is that the cost of such an education is virtually unthinkable to those who subsist on the equivalent of five dollars per day or less.[2] In other situations, such education is inaccessible because there are no institutions near enough to the family home, where obligations preclude significant travel. Even online resources are often not an option, as internet access is poor, expensive, or non-existent. Finally, there are instances where there are simply no established theological colleges or seminaries because a particular government or predominant religious group is hostile to the idea of Christianity, in general. Yet in each of these scenarios, there are presumably some who have been called by God to salvation and some who have received a corresponding call to serve as pastors and elders in local churches.

In many cases, as in Peter's, Christian missionaries have passed through—in the near or distant past—and proclaimed the gospel message. In many cases, also, the Bible is available in the local language. However, if those who have assumed the role of leadership have not had the opportunity to engage in biblical and doctrinal education, they may well be leading their people into error or even into heresy, however sincere their intentions. If, in

---

2. About thirty nations have the equivalent purchasing power (PPP) of US$5.00 per day (Index Mundi).

accordance with one or more of the situations described above, the pastors are unable to obtain formal training, what is their recourse?

Of course, it could be argued that the Holy Spirit can illumine their minds to the truth of God's Word—and this has certainly been true in some instances. However, I have personally encountered such churches where the pastor's theology (and, therefore, the church's) incorporates elements of orthodox Christianity as well as elements of whatever the prevailing religion(s) may be in that culture. The result has often been the denial of the exclusive deity of Christ, the doctrine of the Trinity, and/or other essentials of the Christian faith. Understanding that formal education is clearly the preferable option, nevertheless there is another option that may serve to quell such errors.

This proposal for educational short-term missions (EdSTM) draws on the fact that there are many laymen in the American church who are qualified to teach Adult Discipleship classes in the local church. Further, there are many people in churches in the West who are passionate about missions and the expansion of the global church into the whole world. However, these two groups are seldom seen as companion ministries. I think that they should be. Perhaps those with the gift of teaching have—or may develop—a passion for missions; perhaps those with a passion for missions have—or could develop—the gift of teaching. Such people would be ideal to fill the void among pastors with no access to formal training.

Many American churches sponsor short-term missions (STM). Many times, these trips take short-term missionaries into the poorest areas of the world. These trips are typically promoted as ways to participate in the Great Commission and to share the gospel with those in such dire need. Usually, however, what such trips actually accomplish is less about a gospel proclamation and more about social and/or economic development projects (e.g., building a well, a school, a hospital, etc.) coupled, hopefully, with *relational* evangelism that occurs as the STMers interact with the locals. Of course, there are some such trips that are overtly evangelistic and involve the missionaries in one-on-one street evangelism,

Introduction

evangelistic crusades, and the like. In virtually all cases, however, when the short-term team leaves, the indigenous pastor is not likely to have significantly deepened his own grasp of the faith.

These types of trips usually do not involve in-depth teaching of the local church leaders. This is perhaps because those on the team do not see themselves as qualified to teach; however, the resources that are available to American believers so far exceed what is available to the typical pastor in much of the Majority World that it is only a matter of a commitment of the time and energy for the American to become qualified. Again, there are those who make such commitments regularly when they agree to teach adults in Sunday School. Why not, then, develop a program that will adequately prepare STMers to be able to offer the indigenous pastors a real depth of training on a particular doctrine or biblical theme?

Such a program could be developed at the local church level. Ideally, curricular materials could be developed in the field in conjunction with indigenous pastors. Once the material has been developed, those in the West who feel called to teach and who have a heart for missions could attend preparatory classes until they attain a grasp of the subject matter, in its cultural framework, sufficiently to instruct others.

There are already countless STM models; so, why another one? While it is true that STMs continue to be popular, the majority of these serve the target country with social/health/economic assistance with minimal discipleship applications, as the data in this book will demonstrate. In fact, the most spiritual growth from such trips likely takes place in the life of the missionary rather than in the target culture. This is, of course, an important and valuable element of missions. Any missionary who is not experiencing an ever-deepening relationship with the Lord in the course of his work has likely misplaced his focus. However, there are other ways to promote spiritual maturity without sending people on missions trips! In fact, it is prudent to consider whether the costs associated with such social development trips reflect the best use of a church's missions budget. On the other hand, there can be little doubt that a STMer, properly trained, who can provide substantial training to an indigenous pastor will reap dividends of spiritual growth in that pastor's life, coupled with a corresponding growth in the spiritual life of the church he pastors and, perhaps, extending into other indigenous churches and church plants, as well.

Undergirding this model are two biblical truths: 1) that the church is called to engage in missons as an integral element of its raison d'être; and 2) that those who lead the local church have accepted a weighty and significant responsibility and, therefore, should be adequately prepared to fulfill their calling.

Missions as a Biblical Mandate

Charles Van Engen suggests that evangelical missions should be motivated by "[g]ood news for lost humanity (One Gospel), the Lordship of Christ over his church bringing unity and reconciliation to humanity in Christ (One Race), and the call to set out God's Word in a broken world (One Task)."[3] I would add a teleological component to this theme; namely, to bring glory to God (One Purpose). As John Piper writes, "Missions exist because worship doesn't."[4] That is, the role of missions is to produce true worship which will, in turn, bring glory to the object of that worship: God and God alone. In light of this perspective, the church is called to a focused commitment to glorify God through her active participation in the expansion of His people on earth.

Therefore, the global church should be in the vision of every local church and of every mature believer. There are (or should be) two primary components of this vision. First, the goal of evangelization: calling all men everywhere to repent and turn to Christ (Acts 17:30). Second, and really not materially distinguishable from the first, is the goal of discipling those who are thus converted so that they may be increasingly conformed to the image of Christ (Rom 8:29).

---

3. Van Engen, "Broadening Vision," 214.
4. Piper, *Let the Nations Be Glad*, 17.

Introduction

These twin elements are the sum and substance of the Great Commission, which D. A. Carson notes "is not simply tacked on" as an appendage to the Gospel.[5] In fact, he insists, the Great Commission "brings to a climax" the central biblical theme. This theme, fundamental to the Great Commission, is the idea of mission: the church is to *go*, indicating an active progression of the gospel presentation ever *outward*. Then, once this expanding trajectory is acknowledged, the church is to "make disciples," which inherently includes the conversion aim of evangelism (as the first "step" on the road of discipleship) and to "teach," which typifies the further steps of discipleship, or maturity in the faith (sanctification).[6]

Missiologist Ralph Winter rightly cautions against the misapplication of this mandate, when he notes that, in many cases, "missions has become any Christian volunteering to be sent anywhere in the world at any expense to do anything for any time period."[7] Thus, it is imperative that all missions must have a targeted focus and purpose, such as that suggested in the EdSTM model I propose here.

---

5. Carson, "Ongoing Imperative," 178.

6. The text also includes the command to baptize, of course. Some (particularly those in the baptistic tradition) would see this element of the Great Commission as implicit in the evangelization component; others (particularly in the covenant tradition) might see this element as more consistent with the growth and maturity of the new believer in the discipleship component, with instruction as to the baptism of the believer's household. This is not germane to the discussion at hand and, therefore, need not be addressed at length. It is, however, perhaps worthy of note that such discussions fall squarely under the rubric of the command for "teaching," insofar as each tradition would feel compelled to "teach" the new believers in accord with their own faith traditions. Whatever one may conclude about the content of the baptism command, the fact that it exists—and that it is so fraught with controversy—is further proof that *not* teaching is to fail to properly "equip" the new believers.

7. Winter, "Greatest Danger," 6.

Preparedness for Pastoral Ministry as a Biblical Mandate

It is the role of the church to equip the saints to do the work of ministry (Eph 4:12). One of the ministries for which the saints are to be equipped is the planting of indigenous churches with pastoral leadership that has been called by God and confirmed by godly men (Eph 4:11; Acts 6:3; 1 Tim 5:22). While this call and confirmation are essential and biblically non-negotiable, that is not all that there is in the preparation for ministry; there remains the issue of *equipping*.

Historically, particularly in the Western church since the time of the Reformation, there has been a tradition of pastoral training in a formal context. Another, later stream has co-existed with this tradition: the outgrowth of the revivalist movement on the American frontier in the early nineteenth century. In this tradition, the aforementioned divine call (and somewhat less frequent, the official confirmation) is sufficient to compel a person into the ministry. Further, this tradition has often eschewed formal theological training, as Glenn Miller points out:

> Revivalism demoted the ideal of the learned pastor. Although some sophisticated advocates of the revival used well-developed theological arguments, especially in New England, doctrine was not the mainstay of the awakening. The revivalist moved the heart, not the head, and inspired action, not reflection.[8]

While the merits and challenges inherent in the two positions have been argued elsewhere,[9] this book proceeds on the conviction that for a pastor to be "able to teach" and "able to give instruction in sound doctrine and also to rebuke those who contradict it" (1 Tim 3:2; Titus 1:9), he must be properly educated. This education, however, may be in a formal seminary setting; as an apprentice under the care of a learned mentor; or, as proposed herein, through

---

8. Miller, *Piety and Intellect*, 29. Cf. Marsden, *American University*; Finke, *Churching of America*.

9. See Strange, "Seminary Education." Cf. Frame, "Learning at Jesus' Feet."

Introduction

intensive, targeted instruction in key areas of Bible and/or doctrine within the indigenous context. However it is accomplished, the training of pastors is consistent with the biblical models of replication and multiplication in ministry, such as is evident in Paul's instruction to Timothy: "what you have heard from me in the presence of many witnesses entrust to faithful men who will be able to teach others also" (2 Tim 2:2).

Thus, for Paul, it was given that the theological foundation and framework of ministry be transferred to each new generation of pastors and elders in the church. This is further seen in Paul's continued relationships with the churches he planted, as the epistles are evidence that the apostle was concerned not only with the conversion of souls but with their spiritual nurture, as well. There are even a number of instances where the epistles relate that Paul is sending men back to the churches, for the purposes of teaching, encouraging, and otherwise improving their spiritual condition (2 Cor 8:16–9:5; Eph 6:21–22; Phil 2:25–30). The churches to which these epistles and men were being sent had pastors. No doubt, these pastors' ministries benefited greatly from these resources. Indigenous church plants in the present age also need such resources. While they do have the inspired text of Paul's letters (along with the rest of the Bible), they are often sorely lacking the training that comes only from a teacher who can expound upon the biblical text and assist the pastor in the application of that text in his ministry in the local church. Meeting this need is the purpose of the EdSTM model.

Summary

The Bible makes clear that the idea of missions is integral to the plan of God. Walter Kaiser argues that there is a "missionary mandate" from the earliest pages of the Old Testament.[10] Three passages that support this idea are Genesis 12:1–3, Exodus 19:4–6, and Psalm 67. In Genesis 12:1–3, two points are worth noting.

---

10. Kaiser, "Israel's Missionary Call," 10.

First, God directs Abram to "leave your country." This is an early indicator that God sends (Latin: *missio*) his people. Second, God promises Abram that, in going where God is calling him to go, all the peoples on earth will be blessed. This indicates the universal aspect of the plan of God. Johannes Verkuyl calls this passage "God's election of Israel with His eye on the world."[11] In Exodus 19:4–6, God expresses his particular intent for Israel: to be his "treasured possession," a "kingdom of priests," and "a holy nation." The second of these descriptors, "kingdom of priests," indicates that God is setting Israel in place to mediate as priests between him and the nations of the world. Finally, in Psalm 67, the psalmist, under the inspiration of the Holy Spirit, makes known God's desire to be praised by "all the peoples" as his salvation is made known "among all nations."

The New Testament significantly enlarges and expounds upon the missionary mandate for the people of God. In Matthew 9:37–38, Jesus says: "The harvest is plentiful, but the workers are few. Therefore beseech the Lord of the harvest to send out workers into His harvest." This passage clearly points out the mandate for missions—workers are needed to go into the fields of the world from whence the Lord of the harvest is calling people to Christ. The Great Commission (Matt 28:18–20; Mark 16:15) makes the case explicit: the people of God are directed to go into all the world and make disciples.[12]

The New Testament is, in fact, replete with instances of the missionary mandate. The book of Acts chronicles the concerted effort of the early church to spread the good news of salvation in Christ in concentric circles: first in Judea, and then throughout Asia Minor. The epistles reflect the cumulative effect of the expansion of the Body of Christ through the active engagement of missions. John Stott sums up the missionary mandate quite nicely:

---

11. Verkuyl, "Biblical Foundation," 43.

12. The notion that this directive is for the apostles alone is, in Carson's words, "ludicrous" ("Ongoing Imperative," 179).

Introduction

"We need to become global Christians with a global vision, for we have a global God."[13]

The biblical references to the missionary mandate find their ultimate foundation in the very nature of God. In Ezekiel 18:23, God declares, "Do I have any pleasure in the death of the wicked, rather than that he should turn from his ways and live?" And in Jonah 4:11, he makes known his concern for the people of Nineveh: "Should I not have compassion on Nineveh, the great city in which there are more than 120,000 persons who do not know the difference between their right and left hand?" In these verses, one general and one particular, we clearly see the missionary heart of God.

First Chronicles 16:23–24 exhorts: *Sing to the Lord, all the earth; Proclaim good tidings of His salvation from day to day. Tell of His glory among the nations, His wonderful deeds among all the peoples.* Here, God specifically instructs his people to proclaim the gospel ("good tidings of His salvation") "among the nations," and "among all the peoples," thus making clear that the good news is for the nations of the world. And, here too, the consequence of the salvation of the people is seen to be the outpouring of praise to the glory of God.

In the words of Jesus, Who alone intimately knows the Father's heart, we hear the clear and ringing declaration that God loves the world (John 3:16). The whole of the gospel is, in fact, a testament to this universal love, and the story of the redemptive plan that was put in place to restore lost sinners to Christ. Finally, though many other passages could be cited to show God's great concern for the world, the prayer of Jesus in John 17 is a missiological prayer, showing the heart of God. Jesus prays that believers will be "one" and then explains in verse 17 why this is his desire: "so that the world may believe."

---

13. Stott, "The Living God," 9.

2

The Roots of the American Missions Tradition

In an effort to analyze properly the current state of missions in the American church, it is helpful to consider the development of missions throughout the millennia. While a detailed taxonomy of Christian missions is beyond the scope of this work, what can be assessed are the particular ministries of individual people and larger movements, together with their unique, and often cumulative, contributions to the field. This historical context will assist this study as it considers later the strengths and weaknesses of certain missions practices as they relate, in particular, to the local church and EdSTM in the American context.

Early Church

The "mission" of the church has always been *missions*. The Lord's marching orders to those first assembled on Mount Olivet affirmed as much (Matt 28:16–20; Acts 1:8). Certainly, this was understood at the time, as even a cursory reading of the book of Acts (and most of Paul's epistles, for that matter) makes plain. However, González notes,

> After the New Testament, very little is said of any missionaries going from place to place, like Paul and Barnabas had done. It is clear that the enormous spread of the Gospel in those first few centuries was not due to full-time missionaries, but rather to the many Christians

who traveled for other reasons—slaves, merchants, exiles condemned to work in the mines, and the like.[1]

In fact, for the several centuries after the closing of the biblical canon, there is no discernible pattern of individuals going out into the world with the express purpose of evangelization. That changed in the fifth to the seventh centuries, when the Roman church began to send out monks, who would establish monasteries in various places for the purpose of spreading the gospel. Examples of such endeavors would include Patrick to Ireland (circa 430), Augustine of Canterbury to the Anglo-Saxons (499), and Alopen to China (635).

Middle Ages

Beginning in the eleventh century, as crusaders were sent into lands held by the Muslims at the direction of Pope Urban II and his successors, there was a fresh experiment with missions. At the time, the prevailing view seems to have been that the Muslims were hopelessly lost and not true objects for the Church's evangelistic efforts. They were, in fact, considered "the incarnation of the devil and all heresies."[2] As Neill notes, however, there were a few who held contrary positions, such as Roger Bacon, Thomas Aquinas, and Francis of Assisi.[3] For his part, Francis seems to have been quite convinced that the Muslims could, in fact, be saved and, further, "that the Muslims should be won by love instead of by hate."[4] Francis personally made three evangelistic trips to Muslim lands: to Morocco, Spain, and, lastly, to Egypt. While the first two trips were unsuccessful, the last obtained for him an audience with the Sultan of Egypt, who "listened willingly."[5] Though Francis "made a feeble attempt at sharing the gospel," the language barrier

1. González, *Story of Christianity*, 99.
2. Kee et al., *Christianity*, 267.
3. Neill, *History*, 99.
4. Tucker, *Jerusalem to Irian Jaya*, 57.
5. The Franciscan Experience, *St. Francis and St. Clare*, 1:30.

prevented much in the way of meaningful communication.⁶ The Franciscans (the order of friars devoted to Francis' philosophy) would later choose to employ the simplicity of the gospel and the joy of the Christian life as key evangelistic tenets. This "paved the way for others to view Muslims as potential brothers in Christ."⁷

One such Franciscan, called into the work of missions some fifty years after Francis, was Ramón (or, Raymond) Lull, known as the "Father of Islamic Apologetics."⁸ His interest in learning played a significant role in his missionary strategy. For one thing, he *had* a strategy for missions. Indeed, Neill suggests that Lull was the first missionary to move beyond merely preaching the gospel to considering "in careful detail how it was to be done."⁹

This nascent missiological methodology, as adopted by Lull, consisted of three parts: education and apologetics, in addition to evangelism.¹⁰ Lull was convinced that the missionaries must be able to communicate in Arabic; perhaps here he was learning from the experiences of Francis. Lull set about establishing colleges to train missionaries in the relevant languages and in missions, generally. Regarding apologetics, Lull understood that Muslim scholasticism had resulted in Islamic scholars who expected any debates on the verities of religion to be grounded in reason. Consequently, he purported to do just that, publishing as many as three hundred works.¹¹ These elements of Lull's missiology would become, in varying degrees, engrained in the methodology of missions strategists for centuries. To this day, the importance of learning the local language and the central role of apologetics are core tenets of effective missions models.

---

6. Tucker, *Jerusalem to Irian Jaya*, 57.
7. Ibid.
8. Tennent, *Invitation*, 241.
9. Neill, *History*, 115.
10. Tucker, 58.
11. Tennent, *Invitation*, 242.

The Roots of the American Missions Tradition

Reformation Era

During the tumultuous years from the late Middle Ages to the time of the Protestant Reformation and beyond, there were twin streams of Christianity in play; namely, the Roman Catholic Church and the various Protestant churches. For their part, the Roman church continued an aggressive missions strategy throughout this period, most notably with the monastic orders, such as the Jesuits, founded by Ignatius Loyola in 1534. Loyola sent missionaries throughout Europe, and was instrumental in the formation of a number of educational institutions.[12] With Loyola was Francis Xavier, whom Neill refers to as "one of the greatest missionaries in the history of the church," particularly because of his contribution of "the capacity of the strategist for organization on a large scale."[13] Xavier's mission would take him from Portugal, across India, and, ultimately, to Japan in the East.

With the Catholic efforts moving ahead with such gusto, the work of the Protestants at the time is often thought to be anemic by comparison. It is true that there were not many highly developed strategies among the Reformers to reach particular people groups among the pagan world (though some exceptions are discussed below). Several theories have been brought forward to explain this dearth of global missions. One is that the theology of the Reformers, with its emphasis on the sovereignty of God, led to a dismissive response to the Great Commission.[14] More likely, the cause for the state of Protestant missions in this era was twofold: first, the Reformers were concentrating on the conversion of Roman Catholics, and, second, there simply was no *sodality*, through which a comprehensive missions strategy could be implemented.

Winters defines a modality as "a structured fellowship in which there is no distinction of sex or age," (e.g., denominations).

---

12. Ibid., 444.
13. Neill, *History*, 148.
14. While it is argued herein that the Reformers' theology did, in fact, *not* preclude the notion of global missions, this attitude would develop in time, and would be that against which Carey would prevail.

15

By contrast, he defines a sodality as "a structured fellowship" that requires a "second decision beyond modality membership," (e.g., mission agencies).[15] He also notes that it would be with Carey's famous treatise, *An Enquiry into the Obligation of Christians*, that the idea of sodality would come to the fore in Protestant missiology. Carey proposed "the use of means for the conversion of the heathen." Winters concludes that the word *means* "refers specifically to the need for a sodality, for the organized but non-ecclesiastical initiative of the warm-hearted."[16] Tennent calls this use of *means* "a spark that ignited one of the great *kairos* moments in the history of the church."[17]

The Roman church, of course, had a deep and broad sodality that was all-encompassing: the monastic movement (with its several orders), undergirded by the commanding authority and abundant resources of Rome herself.[18] By contrast, the newly-minted Protestant churches were small, only loosely connected (and then, principally not in a vision of expansion but in doctrinal unity against Rome), and still seeking to define their own role in the world in light of the epochal developments within the Christian faith.

There were, however, important, early "missions pioneers" in the Protestant camp.[19] Among the Lutherans, there developed a movement known as Pietism. In Strasbourg, Philip Spener (1635–1705) began preaching on the importance of the spiritual life through prayer, Bible study, and fellowship. A following quickly emerged and a school was built at Halle. From this university, the Danish-Halle Mission would embark, as Bartholomew Ziegenbalg and Heinrich Plutschau set sail for India in 1705, with "the single

15. Winter, "Two Structures," 247.
16. Ibid., 251.
17. Tennent, *Invitation*, 264.
18. One Catholic historian nicely sums up the benefits of this sodality: "The quality which fitted it for this work [missions] were especially its cosmopolitan character, its faculty of accommodation and mobility, its military organization and centralization, its absolute obedience and the complete submerging of the individual in the common cause" (Quoted in Kane, *Christian Missions*, 141).
19. Sweeney, *Great Commission*, 4.

design of winning [Indians] to Christ."[20] Meanwhile, Spener's godson, Count Nikolas Ludwig von Zinzindorf (1700–1760), also a student at Halle, gathered persecuted Moravians under his protection, all the while sharing with them his own zeal for missions. Soon, these same Moravians would be setting out to share the Gospel in the Caribbean, Africa, India, and the Americas.[21] Though this movement was never large, it certainly played an important role in the developing story of Christian missions, and helped to shape the stage for the work of those who would follow, especially with its emphasis on the spiritual life.

Protestants and the 'Great Century'

Renowned church historian, Kenneth Scott Latourette, coined the phrase, "The Great Century," to describe the nineteenth century, wherein the Protestant churches embraced foreign missions with fervor. [22] He went so far as to devote three volumes of his seven volume compendium, *History of the Expansion of Christianity,* to this era. The names typically associated with this period include John Eliot, William Carey (often called the "Father of Modern Missions"), Adoniram Judson, and J. Hudson Taylor, among others. Norrish suggests that this "great" century was really building upon a foundation lain in the earlier Reformation period, which "represented a fundamental shift in the worldview of Christians; from the medieval tendency to abandon the social world and seek closer union with God (mysticism) to a vision of world transformation in obedience to God."[23] A proper acknowledgement of this foundation is particularly germane to understanding the progressive nature of development within missions.

For instance, while William Carey was certainly an important and significant force in the history of missions, it is perhaps

---

20. Hickson, "Missions," 34.
21. González, *History,* 208–9.
22. Norrish, "Great Century," 267.
23. Ibid., 268.

overstating the case to continue to call him the "father" of modern missions, at least without qualification. As Neill notes, "Carey stood, and was conscious of standing, in a noble succession."[24] This noble succession extends all the way to the aforementioned foundation at the birth of Protestantism in the Reformation; indeed, as has been shown above, the common argument often raised against the Protestant churches in the times immediately following the Reformation are overstated, as well.[25]

As an example, Calvin's Geneva was, in fact, "the hub of a vast missionary enterprise."[26] It is easy to forget that, for the Reformers, the masses of Roman Catholics, in following what was considered a vile heresy, were as lost as the native tribes in the heart of Africa. Hence, for the Reformers, Europe *was* the mission field. Consequently, in France, for instance, there were only five Protestant churches in 1555, but by 1562, following an aggressive program of missions and church planting, there were 2,150 with about three million in membership. Calvin also sent missionaries to other places in Europe, such as Italy, the Netherlands, Hungary, and Poland. An expedition was even organized to Brazil, but the Protestant missionaries were killed on the high seas by Roman Catholics who sought to thwart the expansion of Protestantism.[27] We can see, then, that the evangelistic fires in Protestantism flared soon after the break with Rome and continued, to varying degrees, with the Pietists in Europe and with men such as John Eliot and David Brainerd in America, both of whom "profoundly influenced" Carey.[28]

---

24. Neill, *History*, 222.

25. As an example of such an argument, see James, "Missions Pioneers," 251; cf., Neill, *History*, 222. It is true, as Kane notes, that "the Roman Catholic Church between 1500 and 1700 won more converts in the pagan world than it lost to Protestantism in Europe (*Christian Missions*, 140); however, those "lost to Protestantism" were the result of Protestantism's missionary activity in Europe. What is often decried as a lack of interest in missions among Reformers should be redefined as an interest in a more localized missions target field: namely, the nations of Europe.

26. James, "Calvin and Missions," 23.

27. Hughes, *Pastors of Geneva*, 46.

28. Latourette, *Europe*, 67. There were more besides these two better-knowns;

The Roots of the American Missions Tradition

The oft-overlooked life of John Eliot (1604–1690), known to history as the "Apostle to the Indians," and "a man whom a Pauline spirit had made illustrious,"[29] is central to the study of missions history. For more than fifty years, Eliot labored among the Indians of New England, cultivating a deep love and affection for them, which spurred him on to diligent work in linguistics, translation, evangelism, education, and pastoral ministry. I have written elsewhere,

> Though John Eliot erred in believing that he must make the Indians English before he could lead them to Christ, his mission strategy of preaching the Gospel to them, learning their language and translating the Bible into it, and engaging in a concerted effort to train and establish Indian pastors was, in many ways, a precursor to the work of William Carey and the modern missions movement.[30]

For his part, William Carey (1761–1834) did introduce a new *philosophy* of missions. Neill sums up this philosophy with five distinct precepts: 1) the "wide-spread teaching of the Gospel," carried out through committed "preaching tours"; 2) learning the native language and translating Scripture into it, which Carey and others did to the tune of six full translations and some twenty-three New Testaments within thirty years; 3) establishing a particular church as soon as possible, which the missionaries did in Serampore; 4) a significant study of the local "thought-world," which is exemplified by Carey's Sanskrit grammar and his contribution to Bengali prose literature; and 5) a concerted effort to train indigenous pastors, which Carey undertook with the founding of the college in Serampore in 1819.[31] It has rightly been noted

---

one source notes that Brainerd was "just one of a number of ardent souls who were led by the revival spirit [of the Great Awakening] to become missionaries among the Native Americans" (Kee et al., *Christianity*, 632).

29. Mather, *Magnalia Christi Americana*, 527.
30. Curtis, "Prayers and Pains," 138.
31. Neill, *History*, 263.

that Carey "was no armchair strategist,"[32] and his pioneering work is certainly pivotal—and arguably singularly so—in the story of Protestant missions. In his fervor and determination, and in the implementation of translation work, training, and respecting the local culture, Carey initiated a fresh trajectory in the important work of missions.

Adoniram Judson (1788–1850), the erstwhile Congregationalist turned Baptist missionary, first landed on Burmese soil in 1813. The early years of his ministry were frustratingly devoid of converted Burmese; after six years, there had been only one public profession of faith in Christ, followed by baptism. Yet Judson was not without work. While laboring among the Burmese and evangelizing as the opportunities arose, he was deeply involved in learning the Burmese language. The fruits of this effort were, first, a Burmese dictionary and grammar, followed by brief evangelistic tracts and, finally, the first Burmese translation of the New—and, later, the Old—Testament of the Bible.

Along the way, Judson was faced with innumerable personal crises, such as the deaths of two wives and several children, as well as his own imprisonment for a year under horrid conditions, including torture. He watched other missionaries come and go; some gave up, others were martyred for their faith. Through it all, Judson continued about the work to which he had been called. Before he would die, he would be blessed to see the church in Burma swell to several hundred.[33] In addition to his work of translation, Judson also leaves an important though sobering lesson to the world of missiology: the call to serve is often attended with sacrifice and suffering, and must, therefore, be answered humbly and with an undivided heart.

Another leading figure, J. Hudson Taylor (1832–1905), truly had a magnificent vision from the Lord: he believed that he was called to reach all of China with the Gospel of Jesus Christ. Through his efforts, a mission agency, China Inland Mission (CIM), was organized. Part of the ministry's success was due to Taylor's own

---

32. Kane, *Christian Missions*, 147.
33. Anderson, *Golden Shore*, 415.

personality and character. Also, he had the gift of organization that was so needed in that time and place. Finally, he had the help of his first wife, Maria, in the planning of the ministry, and of his second wife, Jennie, in carrying it out. Still, Taylor was not the first missionary to answer a call to China.

Taylor built upon the earlier work of both Catholic and Protestant missionaries. The Jesuits (and, to lesser degrees, the Franciscans and Dominicans) had at least introduced China to the basic tenets of the Christian faith and, under Emperor K'ang-His in the seventeenth century, the Church had established a foothold along the coast.[34] The Catholics had also utilized the idea of "adopting Chinese dress and culture."[35] Though this practice was not typical of other Protestants, this became a hallmark of Taylor's strategy.

Perhaps more significantly, Taylor also was indebted to the earlier work of other Protestants. Robert Morrison, the first Protestant missionary to China, had succeeded in translating the Bible into the Chinese language.[36] Taylor would also adopt Morrison's position and seek to recruit single women into mission work, rather than men only. Finally, Taylor benefited from the work of Karl F. A. Gutzlaff, an itinerant evangelist who travelled to inland China distributing literature. Gutzlaff had also established the Chinese Evangelization Society (CES), the organization that would eventually sponsor and send Taylor to China in 1853.[37]

While Taylor was able to draw on these influences, he was also committed to an innovative strategy of missions. First, he was committed to a mission that was interdenominational, though united in conservative theology. Second, he was convinced that formal education should not be a prerequisite to missions. Third, after having had unfortunate relationship problems with the CES and forming CIM, Taylor determined that control of the agency should be in China and not across the ocean. Fourth, in keeping

---

34. Neill, *History*, 161.

35. Tucker, *Jerusalem to Irian Jaya*, 189.

36. Presumably this was the ancient dialect, Wenli; see Kane, *Understanding Christian Missions*, 157.

37. Latourette, *Northern Africa and Asia*, 304–6.

with the Catholic practice (and that of Gutzlaff), Taylor insisted that all CIM missionaries would wear Chinese clothes and seek to be identified with the Chinese. Fifth, Taylor was committed to widespread evangelism, with "the shepherding of Churches and teaching" taking a secondary position.[38]

This latter point may have been the weakest in Taylor's strategy. As Latourette noted, "The main purpose of the China Inland Mission was not to win converts or to build a Chinese church, but to spread a knowledge of the Christian Gospel throughout the empire as quickly as might be."[39] This, together with the failure to recruit indigenous pastors and missionaries, perhaps hindered the effect of Taylor's ministry to some degree. It has been rightly said that "God strangely honored him because his gaze was fixed upon the world's least-reached people";[40] still, while Taylor offered several contributions to missions, they are of varying value. His development of the parachurch sodality laid important groundwork for modern agencies, although with the growth of such agencies, there has increasingly been a pull away from the direct involvement of the local church in missions. Perhaps most detrimental of Taylor's practices would be his indifference (if not opposition) toward educated missionaries and his overemphasis on evangelism at the expense of discipleship. It will, in fact, be such errors that contributed to the global missiological problem addressed in this study.

The Twentieth Century

After the turn of the century, the stars in the missions galaxy would not be individuals (as in the previous century), but *movements*. Kane describes three of these, in particular: the Faith Mission Movement, the Student Volunteer Movement, and the Bible Institute Movement.[41] As to the first, these are identified as interde-

---

38. Neill, *History*, 283.
39. Latourette, *Northern Africa and Asia*, 329.
40. Quoted in Tucker, *Jerusalem to Irian Jaya*, 201.
41. Kane, *Christian Missions*, 160.

The Roots of the American Missions Tradition

nominational organizations that "to an unusual degree look to the Lord for the supply of their needs."[42] Kane is here contrasting such organizations with the church-based, or denomination-based, nature of missions prior to this time. Included within this classification would be such notable organizations as Campus Crusade for Christ and Wycliffe Bible Translators. Mulholland suggests that Taylor's China Inland Mission was, in fact, the "prototype" of this movement.[43] These organizations offered the important contribution of a strong focus of faith for God's provision.

The Student Volunteer Movement (SVM) was the result of a paradigm shift away from "the civilizing mission, a vision of a cultural Kingdom of God, and towards the Great Commission."[44] The goal, then, was to plant churches that were self-governing, self-supporting, and self-propagating. This new dynamic was accelerated in the ministry of Dwight Moody and his entrepreneurial evangelism. At a conference held by Moody in Mt. Hermon, Massachusetts, in 1886, Robert Wilder (a supporter of missions from Princeton) challenged the students in attendance to see God's will in the matter of foreign missions. Before long, one hundred students had signed the "Princeton Pledge" saying, "I purpose, God willing, to become a foreign missionary," and the SVM was born, committed to the slogan: *The Evangelization of the World in this Generation.*[45] Among the students who surrendered to the call of missions was C. T. Studd, a highly-touted cricketer, whose father had been converted at one of Moody's evangelistic meetings. Soon Studd, together with six other students from Cambridge, answered the call, and Studd would follow that call, first to China and then to the heart of Africa.

For fifty years, the SVM flourished as more than twenty thousand missionaries went into the field around the world. By the late 1920s, however, the SVM was undergoing a radical shift. Beuttler suggests that SVM's "vision of the gospel . . . blended Christianity

42. Ibid.
43. Mulholland, "Missiological Education," 43.
44. Beuttler, "Evangelical Missions," 114.
45. Kane, *Christian Missions*, 162.

with a broader modern culture . . . which created significant tensions that dramatically transformed the missionary enterprise."[46] The result was that the focus shifted away from the true gospel as the movement became "completely captured by theological liberalism and by preoccupation with social and political issues."[47] Nevertheless, the SVM served a great role in God's unfolding plan for the spreading of the gospel throughout the world, and a number of missionary endeavors (such as Studd's organization: WEC) continue to this day, faithfully leading souls to Christ. The conservative remnants of the SVM gradually evolved into the third movement of the twentieth century, and became interrelated with the faith movement, as well.[48]

The Bible School Movement saw the development of institutes of learning, which were keenly interested in preparing students for missions, as well as instructing them in the Bible. Chief among such institutions would be Moody Bible Institute. Such schools evolved to fill the need, articulated with regret by Mulholland, "that out of five hundred missionary candidates, many had to be turned down for lack of adequate Bible preparation."[49] These schools admirably corrected that imbalance and, ever since, "have sent a steady stream of missionaries to the foreign field."[50] In fact, they sent out such a great "stream" that, in 1985, Kane could write, "1 out of every 16 American missionaries in the world today is an alumnus of Moody Bible Institute."[51] Mulholland, while acknowledging the role of Bible schools, also notes that that model is no longer wholly adequate: "with the explosion of cross cultural missionary activity in the two-thirds world, new models of training are merging which draw from, yet move beyond, the patterns in-

---

46. Beuttler, "Evangelical Missions," 116.
47. Glasser and McGavran, *Contemporary Theologies*, 114.
48. Mulholland, "Missiological Education," 48.
49. Ibid.
50. Kane, *Christian Missions*, 161.
51. Ibid. The trend has continued in the present era: "50 percent of aviation missionaries come out of Moody Bible Institute." http://www.moodyministries.net/crp_mainpage.aspx?id=790.

herited from the Bible College Movement." He goes on to discuss these new strategies:

> The dynamic and practical training programs found among such rapidly growing younger Western-based (but rapidly internationalizing) mission agencies such as Operation Mobilization (OM) and Youth with a Mission (YWAM) bear a striking resemblance to the early Bible institutes rather than the more developed Bible colleges of North America, [and] we are witnessing, particularly among large congregations, the emergence of a new church-based Bible Institute Movement, which has many parallels to earlier training models. [52]

Accordingly, there is, then, a sense of a full circle return to the importance of proper preparation of missionaries. Some of these new sodalities were at the cusp of the newest innovation in missions in the twentieth century: short-term missions.

Short-Term Missions

Today more than 1.6 million adults and young people from the United States travel abroad yearly on short-term mission trips, most for two weeks or less duration.[53] Put another way, "2.1% of all church members in the U.S. traveled on short-term mission trips outside the USA,"[54] and the number shows no sign of letting up. How did this come to be the reality in the church today? Raines rightly notes that attempts to assign a precise beginning for the short-term missions (STM) movement are "vague and varied."[55] Kane suggests that several denominations began using STM in the 1940s, such as the United Presbyterians and the United Meth-

---

52. Mulholland, "Missiological Education," 52.

53. Howell goes on to note that these numbers "do not include high school students, nor do they necessarily track those who have participated through parachurch or college trips" ("Mission to Nowhere," 206).

54. Priest and Priest, "They See Everything," 54. This data was current as of 2005.

55. Raines, "International Perspectives," 11.

odists.[56] Others point to the emergence of sodalities such as OM and YWAM in the 1960s and 1970s as the more accurate date, at least for the type of STM that is now most commonly observed.[57] Certainly, the latter construction more properly interprets the current disparity of *youth* as STMers. At any rate, the success of OM and YWAM led to many more missions agencies—and local churches—incorporating STM into their broader missions strategies. Undoubtedly, the exponential growth of STM can be inextricably tied to the development of two (relatively) modern innovations: intercontinental jet service, which makes far-flung places accessible and, more recently, the Internet, with its ability to make the hitherto formidable cultural divide among people groups seem less distinct, as so many cultures gather around the same social networking sites and interact amongst one another via email, discussion boards, and the like. In a very real sense, these two factors have contributed significantly to *shrinking* the world. It is no surprise, really, that missions strategists would be compelled to at least consider this smaller world in their calculus. Some consider it a benefit; others do not.

For example, modern missions pioneer Ralph Winters lamented the rapid growth of STM, likening it to similar well-intentioned but less than perfectly executed strategies from the past: "One hundred years ago hordes of young people rushed out to the field and did silly, tragic things—and were encouraged by adults back home. That was a massive amateurization of mission. It is happening again."[58] He is not alone in his assessment; many have decried the potential risks associated with the STM phenomena. Some argue that STMers are all too often a burden to the LTMers who have to host them, adding to their already significant workload. Others point to the propensity of STMers to be culturally ignorant or insensitive. Still others are bothered by the thought that scarce financial resources are diverted from LTM efforts to fund

---

56. Kane, *Christian Missions*, 371–2.
57. See Raines, "International Perspective," 12.
58. Ralph Winter, "Greatest Danger," 6.

what many consider little more than Christian vacations.[59] Regardless of the opinions for or against STM, this represents the reality of the current state of missions in the evangelical church. Stan Guthrie offers a helpful summary of STM and the associated risks:

> Short-term work, whether two weeks or two years, can indeed be effective and pleasing to God. Yes, it can cost a lot of money, disrupt nationals and missionaries, encourage short-term thinking, and inoculate some against career missions involvement. But done well, it can open participants' eyes to the sometimes gritty realities of the world, make them aware of their own ethno-centrism and the gifts and courage of non-Western believers, and spark a lifelong commitment to missions. In the best cases, some real kingdom work gets done, too.[60]

Perhaps it is best simply to view STM as "a reflection of local churches' desire to be involved more directly in global mission."[61] In other words, rather than a wholesale dismissal (of something that is not likely to go away anyway), the focus should be on striving to do it well.

Educational Missions

In 1986, Kane wrote, "Two generations ago John R. Mott stated that the greatest weakness of the missionary movement was our failure to produce well-trained leaders for the national churches. Half a century has come and gone and the problem is still with us."[62] In some cases, this is the result of missions endeavors that are heavily weighted toward evangelism and conversion and less so toward church planting and pastoral training. In other cases, this is due to the inaccessibility of formal theological education in the indigenous

---

59. Taylor actually uses the phrases *glorified sightseeing* and *funding vacationaries* to describe this charge often leveled at STM ("Flying," 125).
60. Guthrie, *Missions*, 89.
61. Moreau et al., *Introducing World Missions*, 281.
62. Kane, *Christian Missions*, 324.

context (often simply because of economic restraints). At any rate, this continues to be a significant crisis in the global church.

To be sure, there have been advances in this area, not least of which is Ralph Winter's groundbreaking program, Theological Education by Extension (TEE),[63] which Tennent regards as Winter's "defining moment" as a missiologist.[64] The program offers distance education materials to older, in-ministry church leaders, either in a self-study format or through study centers. The philosophy behind TEE was simply a response to the reality that many if not most indigenous pastors are neither properly educated nor able to pursue theological education in a formal setting. Winter warned that traditional seminaries were quite inadequate to meet the needs of present and potential pastors, noting:

> History and experience have taught us that only a handful of potential leaders ever find it possible to leave their families, their farms and other vocations to spend six or nine months a year in a central Bible school. If we continue to cling to this long-established, highly-cherished pattern of theological education we shall reach only a fraction of the total number of potential church leaders in any country.[65]

TEE developed in the context of Latin America, where Winter served at a time when, "of the 150,000 men serving congregations, possibly 90 percent lacked theological training."[66] By coupling education with ministry, TEE was designed to meet this need. In various formulations, this model has had some success. However, there have been some issues that have challenged the efficacy of the model. First, because it is largely intended as a self-study program, and one easily accessed at that, there exists a real test of the participant's commitment. Also, the model presupposes that someone can serve as a tutor; however, the question arises: who? If a national, how does he gain the knowledge to lead others? In other

---

63. Developed in 1963 with James Emery.
64. Tennent, *Invitation*, 355.
65. Winter, *Theological Education by Extension*, 267.
66. E.H. Wendland, "Theological Education by Extension," 2.

words, who teaches *him*? Conversely, if a Western missionary is to be the tutor, the heart of the model (i.e., avoiding the stereotypical approach to Western-led theological education) is gutted.[67] Thus, this permutation of educational missions is useful, but there are self-imposed obstacles. The stridently observed ideology of TEE supporters, that Western intrusion into the national's theological education should be minimal, produces a crippling blow.[68]

Other forms of educational missions take place every day as missionaries go into the field to provide theological education to indigenous church leaders. Typically, these are pastors or Bible School/seminary professors who go to serve as adjunct faculty in other schools in the Majority World. Others (again, vocationally in ministry) may venture further into the field and convene a group of pastors to be taught in some other format outside of an institutional setting. I have done both: served as guest lecturer in established seminaries and served in villages deep in the jungles or mountains of Africa and Asia. Both are critical.

Summary

The history of the church's efforts to fulfill the Great Commission provides a wealth of data for any new missions paradigm. There are important lessons to be learned from the past. Most missiologists accept the value of many of these lessons, such as the importance of translation, church planting, and contextualization. However, the prevailing short term missions models in America have not adequately addressed the lessons learned from this history with regard to pastoral education. As the opening narrative demonstrated, proper training of indigenous pastors continues to be a great need. It is to the church's response to that need in the present day that this study turns next.

---

67. Kornfield, "Challenge," 13–22.

68. See Kinsler: "Traditional training patterns reinforce the dichotomy between clergy and laity; they debilitate the dynamics of ministry at the congregational level; they make the churches dependent upon highly trained, professional pastors" (*Extension Movement*, 8).

3

The Cry of the Global Church and the American Response

Having considered how the American missions tradition has developed through time, it is pertinent now to assess the effectiveness of the current missions model(s) in meeting the needs of a world largely consisting of people who either do not know of Christ, or who know of him in only an elementary and impoverished way. It is the function of the church to introduce Christ to the former and to disciple the latter to become more mature followers of him. Some of this work is, of course, within the purview of the local church, as the gospel is proclaimed and God's Word is taught. Much of this work, however, is consigned to that particular aspect of the church known as *missions* and, more precisely in the context of this book, *foreign missions*.

First, the church through her work in missions seeks to take the good news of Christ to those who have never heard. This is perhaps the role most often associated with missions. Second, however (and no less important), the church bears the responsibility for the nurturing of those who are thus introduced and brought, by grace, into a saving relationship with him (Eph 4:11–14). This is often accomplished through the planting of churches and the establishment of Bible colleges and/or seminaries in indigenous cultures. In many cases, these efforts reap a great harvest of mature believers in healthy churches, with properly equipped national leaders who are capable of shepherding their flock. In many other cases, however, particularly in the farthest reaches of the Majority World, these efforts are less effective, producing only anemic spiritual growth among believers who are being led by pastors who are themselves but babes in Christ. To some degree, these lackluster results are due to the divided mind within the evangelical community with regard to missions, generally.

There are some who argue that the Western church—especially the church in America—really should not be directing time and energy toward foreign missions; rather, they suggest that there is more than enough of a need to keep the American church engaged domestically; in other words, America *is* the mission field. The classic expression of this view is, of course, the rebuke issued to young William Carey when he dared to argue in favor of foreign missions: "When God pleases to convert the heathen [in foreign lands], He will do it without consulting you or me!"[1] While there may be no contemporary voice so vociferous in its rejection of foreign missions, there are certainly echoes of such thought in both the insular and isolationist attitudes of many American Christians. Jennifer Collins writes, "A survey of Southern Baptist congregations found that foreign missions ranked as least important among seven suggested ministry areas," and another survey revealed that 75 percent of Christian baby boomers "believed the need for missionaries was greater in the United States than overseas."[2] As to the increasingly isolationist perspective of some Christians, John Fisher points out that "a separatist Christian monologue has replaced meaningful dialogue with the world around us."[3] As the church—or more particularly, the Christian—closes off from the world outside, there is a natural disconnect from the needs of that world outside the safety of *home*. For many in the church today, it is a sad reality that there is virtually no contact with anyone outside of the evangelical community.

---

1. Moreau, *Invitation*, 124.

2. Collins, "Short-Term Missions," 318. This same survey concluded that, "in general, Christian baby boomers are more interested in domestic causes than in world outreach" (319).

3. Fischer, *Fearless Faith*, 15.

Others suggest that the Western church's primary concern should be social rather than evangelical; that is, targeting efforts on meeting the humanitarian needs in the Majority World rather than building up the church *qua* church (i.e., the assembly of converts to the faith). This ideological fruit springs from the root of liberal theology and the vine of the social gospel. As Kane wrote twenty-five years ago, "Anthropology and sociology are rapidly replacing theology, with disastrous results."[4] Such a perspective emerges in the various permutations of liberation theology, which directs the focus of the church and of the gospel away from the spiritual realm and toward the earthly almost exclusively. As they interacted with this idea, Glasser and McGavran wrote:

> Theologians of liberation are concerned with but one frame of reference. They look at all reality through the eyes of the poor and the oppressed. Their dominant concern is that the victims of exploitative and dehumanizing social structures be liberated. This dialectic of oppression/liberation stands in sharp contrast to earlier theologies in the long history of the church. Not morality/immorality, reason/faith, law/grace, guilt/forgiveness, but something distinctly new: a focus on one's neighbor rather than on oneself.[5]

Still others say that while foreign missions are important, such weighty tasks should be reserved for those with the proper training: the professionals. For his part, Kane at least suggests this when he says:

> All missionaries, regardless of their area of specialization, should have a *thorough understanding* of missiology, including the history, theology, philosophy, and methodology of missions, non-Christian religions, cross-cultural

---

4. Kane, *Christian Missions*, 85. Ajith Fernando points to the practical outworking of this theological construct when it is disguised as "doing good" with no reference to sin, judgment, or the need for repentance: "I fear that many evangelicals have fallen into Satan's trap of upholding Kingdom values to the diminution of God's call to practically go after the lost and proclaim the gospel" ("Getting Back on Course," 42).

5. Glasser and McGavran, *Contemporary Theologies*, 156.

communications, missionary anthropology, area studies, church planting, etc.[6]

Attaining a "thorough understanding" of this breadth of subject matter virtually demands a targeted advanced degree in missions. While this may still be sound advice for career missionaries, the more pertinent question for this study would be how true is Kane's statement with regard to EdSTM? Further, how has this mindset affected the church's ability (and even her willingness) to address the significant spiritual needs of the global church?

Finally, there are those who are convinced that the non-Western church is doing a fine job reaching out throughout the world with missions; in other words, let *them* reach *them*. Moreau notes the reality of this global expansion of missionaries, writing, "It seems that the evangelical movement has finally caught up with the ecumenical movement in understanding the realities of mission as a phenomenon to and from every continent."[7] As figure 1 indicates, it is true that the non-Western church has taken on a far more substantial role in global missions than ever before, even beginning to dwarf the Western church in the process.[8]

Figure 1: The Rise of Non-Western Missionaries

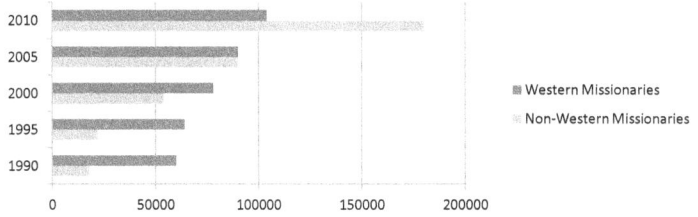

While this is certainly positive from the perspective of the non-Western church (as it is indicative of the proliferation of the gospel in those nations which are sending missionaries into the

6. Kane, *Christian Missions*, 75; emphasis mine.
7. Moreau, *Invitation*, 286.
8. Koch, "Non-Western Mission Force," 370. The data contained in figure 1 are derived from this article.

33

field), the fact remains that three billion people—representing 42 percent of the world—are still unreached.[9] While the non-Western church is to be commended for engaging this very real need, this in no way mitigates the responsibility for the Western church to do likewise. There may be a sharing of the burden, but there cannot be a passing of the baton of missions from the Western church to the non-Western church.

In light of these different approaches to missions, the question remains: are modern missions philosophies and paradigms succeeding in meeting the needs of the church in the Majority World?

Present State of Long-Term Missions

While accurate figures are likely impossible to ascertain in light of the countless independent and/or church-based missionaries, published statistics regarding the missionaries associated with missions agencies are more dependable. Since 1953, the *Missions Handbook* has conducted a survey of the various missions agencies in the United States and Canada to determine a host of statistics.[10] For the purposes of this study, several of these statistical categories are particularly germane.

Figure 2: Distribution of Full-Time Missionaries

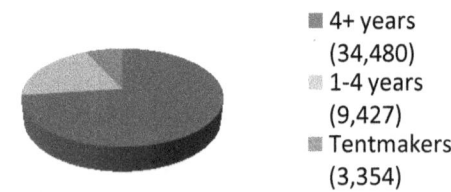

■ 4+ years (34,480)
■ 1-4 years (9,427)
■ Tentmakers (3,354)

Regarding LTM, the *Missions Handbook* reports that there were 47,261 full-time missions workers in the field in 2010. Of

---

9. Joshua Project.

10. Weber, *Mission Handbook*. Unless otherwise noted, all data contained herein are from this source and this edition.

these, 34,480 are committed to service of more than four years, 9,427 are committed to service periods ranging from one to four years, and, finally, 3,354 are engaged in missions work while also engaging in some other vocational trade to support themselves and their ministry (i.e., "tentmakers").

Robert Coote has written, "In a world where hundreds of millions have yet to hear the name of Christ and additional millions have never heard the gospel presented effectively in the cultured context, there is no substitute for the career missionary."[11] He is, of course, correct. The expansion of the Kingdom work requires the committed effort of those who, like the apostle Paul, were prepared to commit to a mission field for an extended period of time.[12] However, the statistics reveal that there simply are not enough career missionaries to accomplish all that is needed around the world. For instance, despite the fact that there are literally scores of missionaries serving in Burma, when I was approached by a group of twelve churches there, it was made clear that no Western missionary had ever ventured into their presence to teach their pastors basic theology. Again and again, the same situation has been revealed in other nations. Quite simply, the demand outweighs the supply. Unfortunately, even the massive wave of STM has not effectively quelled this growing problem.

Two conclusions can be drawn from this data. First, it can rightly be concluded that the long-term commitments of many engaged in vocational missions are generating genuine spiritual growth within individual believers as well as global growth as the Kingdom of God is expanded upon the earth. It may also be concluded, however, that the need is significantly greater than what can be met by the present level of LTM. Many Christians in the Majority World, and particularly many pastors, are crying out with the Macedonians: "Come over . . ." (Acts 16:6–10). In fact, I became involved in EdSTM precisely because such calls—wholly unexpected—came from pastors throughout the world who, aware

11. Coote, "Good News, Bad News," 6.

12. Paul stayed in Corinth for a year and a half (Acts 18:11) and in Ephesus for two years (Acts 19:10).

of their own dearth of theological education, longed to be trained so as to be the leaders that God has called them to be. For them, and for countless others, the needs are simply not being met. Again, on the one hand, the current levels of LTM are insufficient to properly prepare national pastors and, on the other hand, the explosion of STM has not adequately filled that gap. In fact, the focus of STM is more generally toward other work entirely, with pastoral preparation, or educational missions, being far less likely an objective than are social or humanitarian projects, as the data below will demonstrate.

Figure 3: Distribution of Missions Workers by Time Commitment

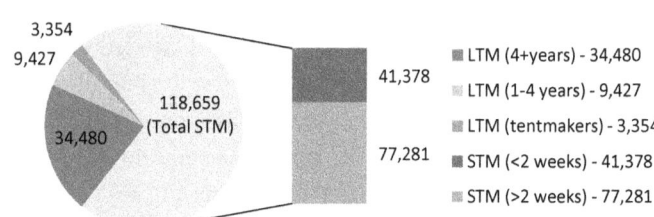

Present State of Short-Term Missions

The net result of the explosive growth of STM has been succinctly addressed:

> As the twentieth century closed, a dramatic shift had taken place. Missionary service was no longer restricted to a career option. Mission trips often were short-term experiences. In the midst of this shift, traditional agencies and churches on the mission fields of the world scrambled to integrate the new wave of volunteers.[13]

That STM has grown exponentially in recent decades is indisputable; that STMers have consequently been integrated into the older missions paradigms is likewise obvious. What is not as

13. Pocock et al., *Changing Face*, 248.

obvious is the actual numbers of STMers in the field today and the role that they are playing in the overall impact of American missions. [14]

Statistical Analysis of STM

While the numbers referenced above reflect a sizable force of LTM, it is a small number relative to the *reported* number of STMers and, most likely, dwarfed by the *actual* number of STMers. With respect to the reported data on STM, the *Missions Handbook* cites missions agencies as having sent out 118,659 STMers in 2010. However, this number is further divided between two categories: 1) greater than two weeks but less than one year, and 2) less than two weeks. Of the total of STMers, 77,281 are committed to serving for a period somewhere between two weeks and one year. That leaves 41,378 who are serving for less than two weeks.

Figure 4: Distribution of All Missions Workers by Task

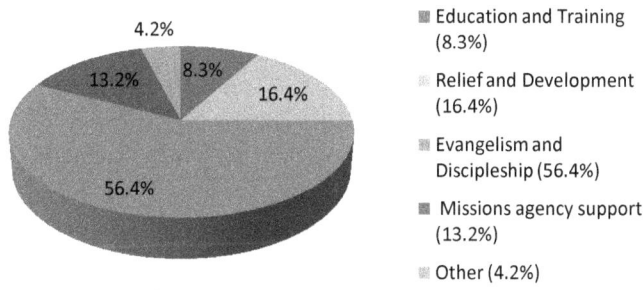

- Education and Training (8.3%)
- Relief and Development (16.4%)
- Evangelism and Discipleship (56.4%)
- Missions agency support (13.2%)
- Other (4.2%)

---

14. The numbers reflected herein are only the product of those agencies who responded to my surveys or to the editors of the *Missions Handbook*. Michael Jaffarian notes that these published numbers "are dwarfed by the explosion of lay short-term mission teams sent overseas directly from churches or Christian schools, most serving for two weeks or less" ("Statistical State," 36).

Taken together with the church-based STMers (discussed below), these figures reveal that the vast majority of American missions activity currently takes place in the context of STM.

What is even more revealing than the *time* being spent in the field are the *tasks* to which that time is applied. The *Missions Handbook* shows that the bulk of all U.S. missions activities (LTM and STM) are concerned with "evangelism and discipleship." This category includes, among other things:

- Bible distribution
- Children's programs
- Broadcasting (radio and/or television)
- Discipleship[15]
- Linguistics
- Literacy
- Literature distribution
- Apologetics
- Evangelism (mass, student, personal and small group)
- Bible translation

Another 16.4 percent of missions workers are engaged in "relief and development" projects. The category of "missions agency support" claims 13.2 percent of those involved in missions, leaving 8.3 percent involved in "education and training." This latter group would include those whose primary focus is in the theological education of indigenous pastors; thus, this is where EdSTM would be located.

---

15. The editor of the *Missions Handbook* does not define "discipleship"; however, as there is a separate category for "education and training," whatever "discipleship" is in this context, is not that.

Figure 5: Change in Mission Foci (2001-2008)

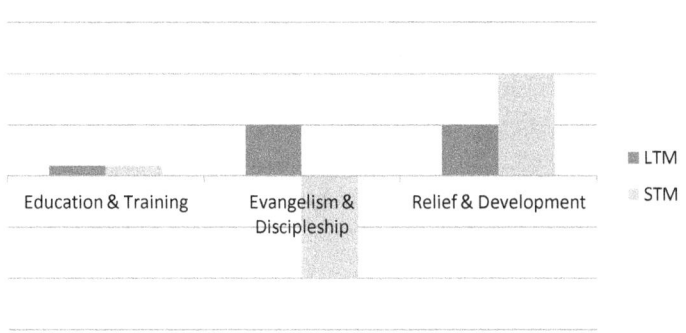

While this would seem at first blush to be a relatively significant number for this area, it is important to note that this number also includes those who are serving in theological seminaries or similar training centers, as well as those who are teaching the pastors in the field.

For instance, I have taught as a visiting professor at both main and satellite campuses of theological seminaries in Asia. The satellite campuses reach a bit closer into the heart of the field, and yet even they remain well beyond the reach of many indigenous pastors, such as those for whom the program proposed herein is designed.

Moreover, the number of STMers dedicated to education and training has grown at only a very modest level over the last decade, whereas the greatest shift has been *away* from evangelism and discipleship and *toward* relief and development projects.

While the *Missions Handbook* reports: "Agencies whose primary activity fits into the education and training category reported solid growth from 2001 to 2008 in the total number of workers deployed . . . ," the analysis continues by noting that the numbers do not reflect "the fact that agencies in this category reported a significant increase in the number of 1 to 2 year full-time workers for 2001 to 2008. The increase from 2005 to 2008 alone was over 600% (from 52 to 367)."[16] Thus, assuming that STM (as it is increasingly

---

16. Moreau, *Mission Handbook*, 53.

identified) are, typically, considerably shorter than the one to two year category that is actually fueling the growth in education and training, the statistics do not indicate a notable growth of STM in the area of education and training.

Further, the summary asserted that "the reported income for overseas work for these agencies [engaged primarily in education and training] dropped almost 29.4% from 2005 to 2008 . . . This may indicate major funding hurdles ahead for agencies whose primary activity focuses on education and training."[17] This would seem to suggest that education ministries have grown as a category of LTM (though even that grouping is apparently facing "major funding hurdles") while showing no discernible growth among STM. Further, because most educational ministries are, in fact, conducted by those in the one to two year grouping, it is reasonable to conclude that these are more likely to be vocational missionaries, often formally educated and trained in the field. The question persists: is this paradigm effectively meeting the needs of the global church?

Survey Data

In addition to the statistical analysis afforded by the *Missions Handbook*, I also conducted surveys among many of the largest U.S. missions agencies, as well as a representative (geographic, demographic, and denominational) sampling of Protestant churches throughout the nation.[18] The results of these surveys reinforced the data discussed above.

The missions agencies surveyed unanimously reported that they make use of both LTM and STM. Most (85 percent) indicated that their overall, primary area of interest was in evangelism and discipleship (especially church planting). However, the bulk of their STM activities are in relief and development categories, with 42 percent involved specifically in construction and 28 percent in

17. Ibid.
18. See Appendix A: "Church Missions Survey" and Appendix B: "Missions Agency Survey."

other "social/economic development projects" (see figure 6). Respondents did indicate that 24 percent of their STM activities were in education and training; however, these same respondents also acknowledged that more than half (65 percent) of their STMers were either actively serving or retired vocational (i.e., ordained) ministers.

Though the survey data does not reveal how many of these ordained STMers are involved in education and training, it is perhaps reasonable to conclude that retired ministers would be more likely to serve in that capacity than youth and less likely than younger STMers to be involved in construction projects. At any rate, anecdotal evidence from the field certainly supports the supposition that the number of STMers who are involved in EdSTM, yet are not vocational/ordained ministers, is demonstrably fewer than those pastors, active or retired, who serve in such a capacity.

Figure 6: Agency-Based STM by Task

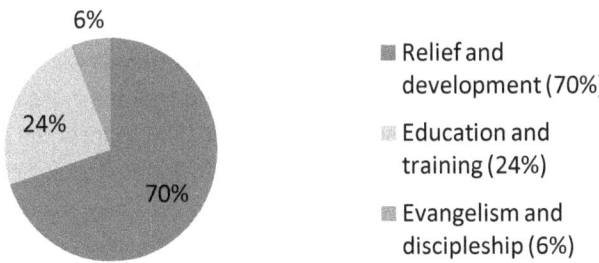

- Relief and development (70%)
- Education and training (24%)
- Evangelism and discipleship (6%)

Data collected from surveys of U.S. churches reveal a similar theme, though with a different balance: more evangelism and discipleship than agency-based STMs, and less relief and development projects (see figure 7). Virtually every church reported that they supported at least one LTM, and however many they supported, the LTMers were involved either in evangelism and discipleship (76 percent) or education and training (24 percent). None reported that the LTMers they support were/are engaged with "relief and development" work.

Figure 7: Church-Based STM by Task

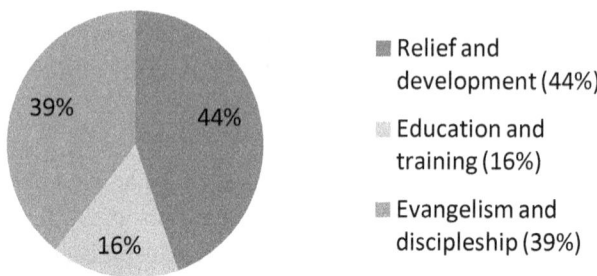

However, while a few (16 percent) reported STM engaged in education or training, fully 83 percent identified their STM activities as being either in relief and development (44 percent) or evangelism and discipleship (39 percent).

The survey data, therefore, present evidence that the current STM paradigm, whether originating from the local church or from parachurch missions agencies, has a minimal focus on education and training. Further, while LTM from both bases are weighted more heavily in favor of the education and training category, the numbers indicate that there is insufficient LTM to meet the global need for proper pastoral preparation. Most churches, of course, are sincere in their commitment to missions. They may believe that the LTM they support are tackling the *heavy* parts of missions (e.g., Bible translation, pastoral education, etc.), while their STM projects are geared—of a necessity—toward the *lighter* tasks, which can be accomplished by most any willing, able-bodied believer; namely, relief and development projects, coupled with relational evangelism. Most often, these "willing, able-bodied" participants are the youth of the church, a phenomenon that merits a fuller discussion.

The Cry of the Global Church and the American Response

The 'Typical' Local Church Response to Missions

As the data discussed above suggested, most local churches have some involvement with missions. Many do support LTM; most, however, are at least engaged in STM. As Koll writes, "Whatever we might think of short-term trips as a way to participate in mission, it is clear that such experiences have become part of, if not the primary focus of, international mission involvement by many U.S. churches."[19] The several attitudes on foreign missions discussed above notwithstanding, the evangelical church in America continues to have a special interest in the global state of the church and the potential for its expansion through missions.

This is why there are countless opportunities for youth, in particular, to engage in short-term missions trips. Many of these are sponsored by the local church, with the youth raising support through car washes, pancake breakfasts, spaghetti dinners, and yard work, among other tasks. The missions objective is often a project in a nearby state or region or, in more ambitious situations, a Latin American country or an island nation in the Caribbean. These objectives usually take the form of a service project, with the goal of building a school or digging a well or distributing mosquito nets and clean drinking water. Along the way, the exuberant youth leaders assure the congregation that the young people will have opportunities to share the gospel with the local people and souls will be won for the Kingdom of Christ; this is often referred to as "relational evangelism." Then, the youth group returns from their trip and, in an often emotionally-charged service, share stories of relationship-building, heart-changing encounters (accompanied by video presentations on the overhead screens of happy locals interacting with the industrious youth). The service adjourns with a warm sense of missions accomplished.

Much has been written about the STM phenomenon, particularly as it has developed as a component of youth ministry in the local church. For instance, Michael Anthony has written about the pros and cons of such typical STM activities as construction

---

19. Koll, "Wolves among Lambs," 93.

projects and "relational ministry projects."[20] Among the pros, he finds that these trips can make missions more accessible to virtually anyone with little to no training or preparation (short of fundraising) and that they encourage interaction between the participants and the locals in the receptor country. Hammering home the cons, however, is Robert Lupton, who writes

> Contrary to popular belief, most missions trips and service projects *do not*: empower those being served, engender healthy cross-cultural relationships, improve quality of live, relieve poverty, change the lives of participants [or] increase support for long-term missions work.[21]

While Lupton's points are sobering and perhaps more often true than not, such a blanket indictment of STM is also, at least implicitly, an indictment of those who participate in STM. Most such participants believe that they are doing good, even if, as Lupton suggests, the fruit of their labors do not measure up to their expectations. One writer suggests that the "main reason most Christians go [on STM] is to satisfy a desire for an emotional experience which they equate with "being close to God."[22] Perhaps it is this inward focus as originator that results in a terminus similar to what Lupton describes. Or, as another author writes, STM may simply have become "a means to give to ourselves and call it missions."[23] Such a sense of self-serving is surely not the *conscious* motivator for all STM; however, if the admittedly laudable goal of personal spiritual growth overshadows the genuine needs in the field, even if subconsciously, then the mission cannot be said to have been a true success—or at least not a *complete* success.

To be sure, often the young people are wholly committed and eminently sincere in their passion to tell others about Christ; and, to be sure, there are certainly lives that are eternally changed because of such encounters. Again, however, more likely than not, the

20. Anthony, *Missions Boom*, 51.
21. Lupton, *Toxic Charity*, 15-16; emphasis in original.
22. Widner, "Short-Term Missions Trips," para. 18.
23. Cook, "Intercultural Sojourns," 57.

lives being changed are not those of the native peoples but those of the youth who are visiting them. It is a powerful experience to walk into a foreign culture for the first time and see poverty and hunger and disease on a scale that the cable television programs could never accurately convey. It is indeed a humbling and soul-searching experience to be confronted with one's own blessings (and even excesses) when faced with the reality in which most of the world lives. Still, the question must be asked: is this missions model the answer?

On the one hand, there is nothing wrong with the sincere young person (or older person, for that matter) who is compelled to survey his own gracious gift of life in light of objective reality, to understand the significance of counting one's blessings. In fact, any opportunity that encourages people—particularly people in an affluent, entitlement culture—to assess critically the stark contrasts between their lives and the lives of those less fortunate is a good thing. Some may even say that it is a *great* thing, paving the way, as it does, for greater clarity in a person's vision of the world from a biblical perspective. Still, is this what missions is all about? Or, put another way, is this *all* that missions is about?

The obvious answer would be "no." The obvious answer would acknowledge the fundamental aspect of missions—indeed, the *most* fundamental aspect—which is concerned with the propagation of the gospel with the aim of making disciples of Christ in obedience to the Great Commission. The obvious answer is that the local church needs to be concerned with the expansion of the global church, and this involves more than evangelism. It requires the raising up and equipping of pastors to lead the indigenous churches that spring up in the wake of evangelism. Yet, despite it being so obvious, the church has demonstrably failed in effectively addressing this fundamental function of missions: pastoral preparedness for ministry.

Traditionally, two approaches to this problem have been followed. Some believe that this issue should be addressed by sending out large numbers of vocational missionaries; however, the statistics show that there are simply not enough vocational missionaries willing to go. Another option is the development of Bible colleges and seminaries in the Majority World; however, such projects represent an economic obstacle for the poorest of pastors who may want to attend. Nevertheless, both of these are important and viable options to be heartily encouraged, as are exploring and developing open source, no-cost training materials and resources, either in print or online. One final option remains, however, and that is to send non-vocational missionaries into the Majority World for short terms to teach pastors the fundamentals of the faith.

The Need for Educational Short Term Missions as Assessed in the Field

For the specific purposes of this study (i.e., theological preparedness of indigenous pastors), the best way to determine the effectiveness of American missions models is to ask national pastors in the Majority World if they have received/are receiving what they need in this area. Through a series of interviews with ten such pastors and/or church leaders, I have been able to ascertain a sense of the current level of unmet need in this regard. These pastors are nationals from Uganda, Burma (Myanmar), the Philippines, India, Nepal, and Ghana. One of these interviews was conducted via email (Ghana); the rest were conducted in person in their respective countries. The interview questions were generally concerned with 1) assessing the pastors' interaction with Western missionaries and 2) the availability of theological education in their country or region.[24]

As to the first point, each of the respondents noted that he had, in fact, worked with missionaries in his own country. Most had experience with Western missionaries coming to their country to engage in relief and/or development projects. Among other experiences, one (Uganda) had known a missionary from Europe who had led a local team doing Bible translation work. Another (Peter, from the Philippines) had been converted to Christianity as a result of a missionary's evangelistic crusade.

---

24. See Appendix C: "Pastor's Interview Questions and Responses."

As to the second point, four of the ten had attended formal theological training (one each from the Philippines and Ghana, and two from Burma): three in his own country (all but one from Burma), the other in another country in the region. All but two had studied under a missionary engaged in EdSTM; five with me in that capacity.

Digging more deeply into the pastors' thoughts about the interaction between Western missionaries and theological education (i.e., EdSTM), they unanimously expressed a positive reaction. In this regard, the pastors fell into one of three camps: 1) those who had attended formal theological education and had also studied under EdSTM; 2) those who had not attended formal theological education but who had studied under EdSTM; and 3) those who had neither attended formal theological education nor studied under EdSTM.

The first group offered a helpful analysis of EdSTM vis-à-vis formal theological education. While it can certainly be stipulated that formal theological training offers more *time* for learning, it was the conviction of at least this group that the *quality* of the learning was comparable. One pastor suggested that this was due to the fact that the Bible college courses he had taken would only meet for a hour a day for three days a week, compared with his EdSTM experience wherein the group spent almost a full forty-hour week studying together on a single subject. Further, this pastor noted that his EdSTM experience was more personal because the group was smaller than the college class. Also, he felt as though the EdSTM instructor, having spent all day with the group (including lunch and tea breaks every day) developed a closer personal relationship with the group members.

The second group, who had only EdSTM training, also had quite positive comments about their experiences, sharing similar insights as did the first group. They noted that they, too, believe that they acquired significant knowledge in their EdSTM workshop, and that this enabled them to be better equipped to minister in the context of their local church. The final group, having had no real theological training, shared their frustration with their own lack of preparation and their desire to remedy that however possible. While they would certainly appreciate the opportunity to study formally, they acknowledge that this is not a realistic expectation at the present time; therefore, they eagerly encourage those involved in EdSTM to come and minister among them.

All of the pastors interviewed, then, were in substantial agreement as to the inherent value of EdSTM. While some may prefer traditional theological education, and while others may prefer a blended approach that incorporates both traditional theological education and EdSTM, the point of comity for all is that EdSTM provides a valuable resource that is desirable in their context. In each situation, the pastor(s) admitted to a lack of sufficient pastoral preparation among the national churches. Thus, there is a legitimate need that remains to be adequately addressed by either Western or non-Western missionaries, whether LTM or STM.

Summary

If the need for an educational component to missions is so great; if there are not enough LTMers to meet that need; and if the church has already embraced a missions model wherein a host of STMers travel the world (albeit engaging in activities that may or may not be effecting any lasting and/or significant change), perhaps it is time to reevaluate the current missions paradigm, at least as it pertains to church-based STM. Perhaps local churches in the United States would better serve the Great Commission if they were to encourage their members to consider investing the time and effort into becoming equipped to go into the missions field for short visits with a specific, targeted objective; namely, to provide training for the indigenous church leaders. While this may seem like a task beyond the scope of the average (not mega-) local church missions department, it is my conviction that such a proposal is both reasonable and attainable. Rather than simply disparaging existing missions models, we will turn now to a practical proposal for a solution to the missions problem of ill-prepared national pastors: educational short-term missions as a ministry of the local church.

4

Developing an EdSTM Ministry in the Local Church

Having demonstrated that there remains a critical need for the education and equipping of indigenous pastors, I will now propose a church-based missions ministry model designed to meet this need. The core of this model involves using lay volunteers from American churches[1] to work with indigenous pastors to create resources that can be used to train other pastors and the churches in the field of service, at large. This idea may best be illustrated using a railway model:

Figure 8: EdSTM Model

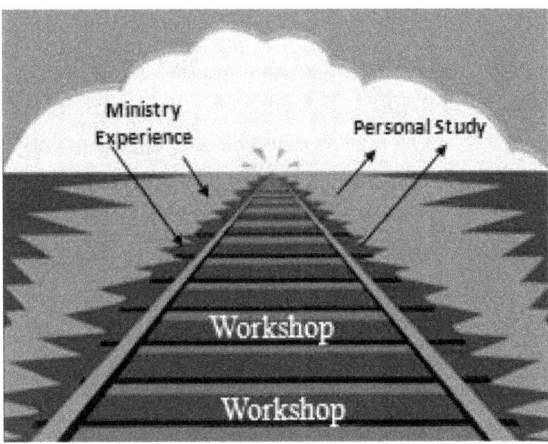

---

1. While this model is specifically designed with the American church in view, it is certainly adaptable to any local church or even group of churches.

Theological Education by Extension (TEE), which was discussed above, is often represented by a similar model, which has been modified here (Figure 8) to better reflect the objectives of EdSTM. The rails represent the indigenous pastor's primary means of learning: 1) personal study of the Bible and supplementary resources; and 2) personal experience in the ongoing work of the ministry. The rail ties represent the EdSTM workshops, where the EdSTMer can enter into a relationship with the indigenous pastor to assist the pastor in bridging the gap between the two rails. Flowing from the middle to the right (in the model), the workshops are designed to better inform the pastor's study with sound biblical and theological training so that his ministry will be more effective. Likewise, the pastor's experiences in ministry will inform his participation in the workshop (from the left to the middle), as this brings cultural context to the development of the workbook(s) discussed below in step 2. The remainder of this chapter will progress through every step necessary to successfully achieve this relationship, based upon the model several others and I developed and implemented through the ministry of Timothy Two Project, International (TTPI).[2]

Step 1: Leadership

Integral to the successful integration of EdSTM into a local church's missions paradigm are leaders who are committed, informed, and prepared. First, these leaders must be committed to the (presumably) new process of training participants in educational missions, together with the logistics that are involved in any STM endeavor. Second, these leaders must be informed with regard to the cultural context of the target field(s), any exigent needs present in that context, and the current level of theological education amongst the pastors in that field (if any). Finally, such leaders must be prepared

---

2. Cf. http://www.timothytwo.org. While TTPI is a missions agency (and not a church-based missions model, per se), it was conceived as a "church-friendly" model that can be managed entirely within the local church.

to engage in research, training, oversight, and logistics. Where would the typical local church find such leaders?

Most local churches have some formulation of a missions ministry and a discipleship ministry. Granted, these may not be well defined, and they are often not staffed positions, but there is usually someone who is responsible for whatever missions the church is engaged in, and there is usually someone else who is responsible for the Adult Discipleship (AD) or Sunday School programs. This model would be most effective if these two leaders/ministries were able to combine their strengths and resources.[3]

First, the person responsible for the church's missions activities would be best equipped to ascertain the right field of service, in light of that area's particular needs. Also, this person would have at least some experience (or would likely be receptive to gaining some experience) in the training, sending, and debriefing of STMers. Most importantly, this person would surely have a heart for the expansion of the global church, and a passion to see the fulfillment of the Great Commission. Thus, this person would be essential to the propagation of an EdSTM ministry.

Second, however, and equally pertinent, would be the person responsible for the oversight of the church's training program for adults. Again, whether this is called Adult Discipleship or Adult Sunday School, most local churches have some program in place that allows adults in the church to study books of the Bible, various practical topics, or even theological concepts during an hour or so before or after the Sunday morning worship service. What's more, these programs usually rely upon the members of the church to conduct these classes. Often, these teachers are laymen who simply have a passion for discipleship—a desire to see other believers grow deeper in their walk with the Lord. They usually have some gifting appropriate to such a calling, such as being comfortable

---

3. It is unknown what would be a base requirement as to the minimum size of a local church desiring to pursue an EdSTM ministry; however, it is reasonably assumed that the smaller the church, the greater the weight of responsibility upon the person(s) tasked with implementing the program. In extremely small congregations, this weight may prove untenable for whomever it would fall upon.

speaking in a group setting, being astute at formulating and communicating ideas, and interacting with a somewhat diverse group of people. The leader of this ministry could provide guidance to the potential EdSTM participants, with regard to the development and preparation of the curriculum to be used in the field.

Together, then, these two individuals could contribute the necessary leadership to facilitate a missions program that is 1) concentrated on discipling other believers through 2) a teaching format in a foreign context. To be sure, the missions director may never have considered the prospect of organizing a targeted educational program in the field; neither may the discipleship director have envisioned implementing a teaching program far from the comfortable walls of the church's educational wing. Still, by uniting their gifts and callings, these two people—in positions common to most local churches—could serve together to create the heart of an EdSTM ministry in their church.

Finally, this ministry would require the enthusiastic support of all of the church's leadership. Pastors and elders would have to *catch the vision*, and see the potential for life-changing ministry in EdSTM. They would have to encourage flagging confidence in the prospective teachers; they would have to motivate the missions and discipleship directors to operate outside of their comfort zone; and they would have to rally the local Body of Christ to mount a prayer campaign that would cover the planning, training, and execution of the EdSTM.

Ultimately, the church as a whole would have to be on board with such a radical notion as EdSTM. Everyone would have to be included in the process—from participating in trial runs of the curriculum to offering additional financial support (if needed) to fund the trips. This may seem like an immensely challenging task; however, the church that is genuinely committed to serving Christ will always be eager to see his Kingdom expand upon the earth. The church that is hesitant or tentative in this regard may well be revealing its own weaknesses. This is not to say that undertaking such a task is *not* challenging; nevertheless, the church that truly has a singular desire to follow Jesus will follow him wherever he may lead. It is, after all, *his* leadership that is paramount in this and any endeavor; any other, earthly leadership is simply reflective of an obedient and willing heart, consecrated to his purposes. Surely the local, evangelical church has such leadership prepared to serve the Master; they may just need to be discovered.

Step 2: Materials/Resources

Once the leadership is in place to begin planning EdSTM in the local church, the next step is to consider the materials that will be taught in the field. I have found that the materials available in most Majority World contexts, outside of formal theological schools (and sometimes even then) are of two kinds: they are either culturally disconnected or theologically deficient. As to the former, most materials available in the Majority World have been given by well-meaning people and organizations in the Western world. Often, missionaries, churches, or other organizations hear of a particular people group's need for pastoral or theological education, and they generously donate books or other resources intended to meet that need. While these gifts are, again, well-meant, they often fail to accomplish the objectives of the benefactors—and that, sometimes, horribly so. For instance, I know an indigenous pastor who made such a need known on an online discussion forum. Some other forum participants pooled their resources and sent a box of teaching CDs to this pastor. Unfortunately, he had no access to a CD player or a television; and the availability of electricity was sporadic, at best. While this is an extreme example, it reflects a common theme: pressing Western cultural norms onto a culture that is wholly foreign to them.

In the case of books and other written materials, the problems are similar. Most Western-crafted theological resources are, understandably, written with a Western audience in mind. This creates two distinct problems. First, there is the (perhaps subconscious) tendency to assume that Western illustrations are comprehensible in the Majority World. However, talk of iPads or smart phones, skyscrapers or subways, or even supermarkets or restaurants, is lost to people who live their entire lives on a savanna in Uganda, in a jungle in Burma, or on the mountainous slopes of Nepal. Second, there is the doubtlessly unintended dilemma of teaching beyond the comprehension of the locals. Many of the pastors clamoring for theological education are poorly educated, with many being barely literate. A theological text designed for seminarians—or even for high school Bible students—is simply incomprehensible to many in the Majority World.

The other side of the problem arises when the local churches in the Majority World develop their own resources. Certainly, these materials are far more culturally relevant and are more easily grasped by the people; however, the authors of such resources can only write of what they themselves know. If they are not properly trained, their material products will reflect this. If, for example, the local pastor has fundamentally confused the concepts of *works* and *grace* (as I have witnessed on many occasions), his whole body of work will be compromised. Pastors such as these may be diligently teaching the people under their care, but they are diligently teaching errors to them. As a result, there is not only no forward progress toward spiritual maturity, but there is often a regression to an earlier juxtaposition of Christian faith with superstition or folk tradition. The end can be troubling, indeed.

Of course, there are exceptions. Of course, there are pastors in the Majority World who have a firm grasp of weighty theological concepts. There are many, in fact (such as those discussed in chapter 3), who have had the opportunity to attend formal theological training. These are not, however, the ones for whom this proposal is intended. This system of EdSTM is designed specifically for those indigenous pastors who do *not* have such opportunities, who have little more than a Bible, a church, and a call.[4] How will *they* learn?

---

4. At this point, it does little good to issue challenges to the validity of a call that is not attended with proper training; the reality is that these men *are* pastors, they *do* have spiritual oversight over people, and, therefore, they *must* be properly equipped.

Developing an EdSTM Ministry in the Local Church

The resources, then, that EdSTM requires consist of two principle elements: orthodox doctrine and cultural contextualization.[5] The local church's director of discipleship can likely help put together the orthodox doctrine for the curriculum, and the missions director may even be able to help with the cultural context to some degree. The real contextualization, however, comes from within the context itself—within the receptor culture.

The model I have employed has been to develop workbooks that carefully yet simply present essential doctrines, together with the body of biblical references to support them. The EdSTMer then takes these workbooks into the field of service where, with the aid of the indigenous pastors, additions are made to it. For instance, the local church leaders can add illustrations helpful in teaching the doctrine, as well as discussion questions that will serve as teaching aids when he begins to utilize the finished workbook in his own ministry. Two goals are accomplished with this model: first, the indigenous pastor is himself educated in the doctrine by the EdSTMer during the workshop, and, second, he is equipped to teach that same doctrine, as well. These workbooks should represent a cooperative effort between the missionary, who ensures doctrinal accuracy, and the indigenous pastor, who contributes cultural context, with the result being an orthodox yet culturally relatable resource.

As for the subject matter of the workshop, the needs in a particular field of service will be a significant factor, although the basics of systematic theology, together with biblical surveys, will typically be useful in most such environments. It is possible, however, that an indigenous pastor will have a solid grasp of some aspect of doctrine and have a greater need in respect to another aspect. Thus, the workshops should reflect the unique needs of a particular context, which can only be ascertained by interacting with people within that context from the outset.

---

5. See Step 6 below for more details in this subject.

Step 3: Discerning the Field of Service

Even before a church in the U.S. can decide what subject to prepare for a EdSTM workshop, and, in fact, even before they can begin to develop an EdSTM ministry with any degree of earnestness at all, there must be a time of prayerfully seeking the guidance of God in determining the field of service where he would have the local church become engaged. In fact, the church must insure (if it has not already) that it is God's will for them to pursue EdSTM as a ministry. George Miley reminds the church of the importance of seeing the "big picture," even when planning a short-term project, noting that "any short-term activity finds its greatest value when it exists, not for its own benefit, but as an integral part of a long-term process."[6] This "long-term process" must be at the back of any prayerful deliberations a church and its leaders have with regard to EdSTM.

It is a good and godly objective indeed that seeks to equip pastors in the Majority World to be more effective in their ministries; it is a great and God-honoring objective, however, that looks beyond the act of simply equipping, and plots a desired end—not only for the pastors' own spiritual formation, but for the expansion of the kingdom, as those pastors teach others, who then plant churches, become missionaries or pastors, until the day of the Lord. In other words, the church that is considering EdSTM and is asking God to lead them to the right people group must take care to adopt God's mission as well as his immediate will: the church must ask itself, "How can we be used to the glory of God in the world?" Then, if the answer continues to be connected with the idea of training pastors in the field, the work can progress; but not before.

Once the church is convinced that they are, in fact, called to pursue EdSTM as an outreach ministry, there are sources available that can assist in the critical stage of discerning a field of service. Perhaps the greatest resources presently available to learn about the people groups around the world are *Operation World* and the

---

6. Miley, "Awesome Potential," 747–8.

Joshua Project.[7] *Operation World*, begun by two missiologists from WEC International, annually produces a sourcebook that gives details about virtually every people group around the world, with respect to the need for missions. In recent years, the basics of this material are also available on *Operation World*'s website, where a user can click on a particular nation and view interactive maps and learn the details regarding indigenous people groups, predominant religion(s), and the degree of evangelical presence. Though the print resource provides this data in much greater detail, the website can serve to pique the church's interest in and passion for a region, nation, or people group.

Linked to the *Operation World* website is the *Joshua Project*, with its focus on those people groups where there is little to no evangelical presence. Founded in 1995 with the particular vision to be a "research initiative seeking to highlight the ethnic people groups of the world with the fewest followers of Christ,"[8] the *Joshua Project* is now aligned with the agency founded by Ralph Winters: the U.S. Center for World Missions. This ministry offers a wide variety of technological gateways to their data, from an interactive website to mobile applications, and SMS and email digests highlighting for prayer the "Unreached People Group of the Day." A church wishing to discern a field of service for EdSTM can perform a search on the *Joshua Project* website, based upon a number of criteria such as: "population, geographic area, religion, status, ministry resource availability including Bible translation status, the Jesus Film, and Gospel audio recording."[9] These search parameters are particularly helpful if the church has some connection to, or relevant interest in, ministering to people in certain regions, religions, and so forth.

In addition to these two ministries, local churches can access a host of potential missions data from the *World Christian Database* from Gordon-Conwell Theological Seminary,[10] *Ethno-*

---

7. http://www.operationworld.org/; http://www.joshuaproject.net.
8. http://www.joshuaproject.net/joshua-project.php.
9. Ibid.
10. http://worldchristiandatabase.org/wcd.

logue[11] (a detailed reference of all of the languages of the world), or the *People Groups* website of the Southern Baptist Convention's International Missions Board.[12] There are, of course, a number of other resources and references that can assist a church in their search for where God would have them engage in EdSTM, not the least of which may well be a church or team member's personal interaction with a people group through friends or relatives. All such resources should be considered in the church's search for a field of service.

Integral to such a search are two elements: 1) assure that the targeted field of service *does* have at least some evangelical presence (as EdSTM is not an evangelistic ministry, per se, but is concerned, rather, with equipping existing churches); and 2) assure that the targeted field of service does *not* have ready access to qualified biblical and theological training already. This latter point demands qualification. There may well be a solidly evangelical and financially-accessible school or training center in a particular region or nation; however, this center may not be accessible to every people group in that region or nation. In some societies, race or caste divisions aggressively persist even among evangelical churches. Thus, a training center may be accessible to one tribe or ethnic group and not another. The reason for this may not even be racial exclusion necessarily, but simply that the tribal groups may not communicate with one another and, consequently, one group may not even be aware of such a training center. In other instances, however, deep-rooted suspicions of other tribes are indeed a sad, divisive factor. There may also be a seminary with very modest tuition rates; however, even the lowest of rates may be beyond the reach of some. Thus, this provision is not intended to exclude a people group simply because of what those around them can access in the way of theological training; it is, however, intended to make the best use of limited resources by targeting those with *no* access to theological training

11. http://www.ethnologue.com.
12. http://www.peoplegroups.org.

Developing an EdSTM Ministry in the Local Church

To best understand this distinction, "field of service" should be understood not to refer simply to geographical space, but to cultural and/or socio-economic space. That is, there may well be a legitimate field of service in an impoverished corner of a large metropolis in a Majority World nation. My work in Burma is a fitting example of this, where the EdSTM participants stay in a small village less than an hour's drive from the heart of Yangon with its four million residents. Yet for the villagers, who are impoverished even by the standards of the Majority World, the resources of the city are far beyond their reach. So, then, are the handful of theological seminaries in Yangon not accessible to them, making this an appropriate field of service for EdSTM.

This same principle can even be extended to the sphere of technology. Simply because Internet access is available in a city (such as Yangon) does not mean that it is available to everyone in that city. In many countries in the Majority World, the Internet remains wholly foreign to large segments of the population.[13] This is simply due to the economics of priority: such families are often faced with a choice between food and electricity in their ramshackle homes. Or, in the case of those that can afford both food and electricity, they may have to choose between a telephone line or medical care (dial-up Internet remains the most common connection in the Majority World; broadband or wireless signals are still fairly rare).[14] Thus, simply because there are myriad theological resources available online, often at no cost, the cost of Internet access itself is so high as to render that a world out of reach. This is why EdSTM is such an important tool in meeting a vital need, and this is why the proper selection of a targeted field of service for EdSTM is so critical. Once these criteria are met, the next step is to narrow the remaining options to a small handful—about 3-5 possibilities—and then take the necessary time in prayer, as a team

13. For instance, only an estimated 28.6 per cent of Africans and 40.2 per cent of Asians have access to the Internet; see Internet World Statistics.

14. Even in the United States (as of 2011), only 43% of households with annual incomes below $25,000 had broadband access at home; http://www.networkworld.com/community/blog/us-snapshot-broadband-world-finds-disparity-a.

and as a church, to seek God's will as to which way to proceed. When the field of service has been selected, the team must seek a partner in that field.

Step 4: Developing a Relationship with an Indigenous Pastor

Having determined that it is God's will for the church to proceed with an EdSTM ministry, and having determined his will for the area where this is to take place, the next step is to locate and contact a local pastor in that field.[15] It is at this point that the project begins to take on a less abstract and more personal tone, as the discussions move from people groups and nations to a person with a name. This shift to personal relationship carries with it all of the elements of building any relationship and interaction, of course, but it also has unique elements that the team must consider and evaluate. In addition to cultural, language, and even economic divides, there are issues that can derail a ministry virtually before it even gets started.

It is a sad but true reality that many relationships between missionaries and indigenous pastors are not always idyllic. Often, there are unrealistic presuppositions on either side. Cook and Van Hoogen correctly identify some common objections to STM, generally, which are also applicable to EdSTM. One of these is that "many receiving churches are only in it for the economic benefits" or "for what the visitors leave behind."[16] While this may seem at first blush to be a rather harsh indictment of otherwise genuinely committed Christian leaders, it reflects the widespread perception among those in the Majority World that Westerners (and Ameri-

---

15. It is, of course, possible that this step will precede the previous steps; that is, an indigenous leader may already be known or may become known before the church begins to even consider the development of an EdSTM ministry. However, the order herein represents the logical path for the church that is unaware of a particular need with a particular people group, but wishes to begin an EdSTM ministry, nonetheless.

16. Cook and Van Hoogan, "Short-Term Ministry," 54.

cans, in particular) are wealthy. It is true, of course, that the average American enjoys a standard of living far greater than that of the typical person living in say, Uganda or Burma, and yet it is equally true that this average American does not have an unlimited supply of resources, either.

Anecdotally in this regard, I recently served as an EdSTMer in an Asian nation. In anticipation of this visit, the indigenous pastor was asked what would be needed to make adequate preparations, to which he replied: "Ten thousand dollars"! He simply had no concept of either how much funds are really required (for five days of expenses for a group of about seven people meeting in a church building) or of how much ten thousand dollars really is. For a man who earns little more than the equivalent of a dollar per day, virtually any sum is unimaginable. Further, I was to be the first Westerner ever to visit this particular village, and the pastor later confessed that he had begun to have visions of this visit resulting in new church buildings, electronic equipment, and even a fleet of vehicles to collect prospective church attendees from the surrounding mountains! The problem was not in his desires (none of which were for his personal gain), but in his *expectations*. The American church seeking to establish a working relationship with an indigenous pastor in the targeted field of service must take care to identify what that pastor should reasonably expect from the relationship, and what he should not expect. After I clarified the nature and purpose of the visit—and the limited funding available for it—the EdSTM was able to be conducted effectively and with the pastor's wholehearted agreement to the targeted scope of the ministry. Once he fully understood what he *could* expect to gain from the visit, he was not as concerned with *not* getting that which he could *not* reasonably expect.

While the failure to address adequately the nature and scope of the proposed trip can lead to confusion and hurt feelings, so too is the not uncommon problem related to the "insensitivity of guests who impose their agenda on their hosts."[17] In other words, there are situations where the missionaries arrive in the receptor

17. Ibid, 55.

culture with the conviction—often borne of their genuine love and concern for the indigenous church—that they bring with them all of the answers. That is, the Westerners, even if subconsciously, present themselves as arrogant and insensitive in light of unique cultural elements that are foreign to them. It is true that one advantage of EdSTM over STM models of intentional or relational evangelism is that the audience (the indigenous pastors) is already convinced of the truth of the gospel and hungry for it; consequently, he is less likely to be offended to the point of disassociation when the Westerners inadvertently trample over some tradition or cultural practice in their zeal to *fix* the problems of the indigenous church. However, it is unrealistic to assume that such offenses have no effect whatsoever and, in that effect, are not detrimental to the overall effectiveness of the mission. This is why Bob Creson, the president of Wycliffe USA, cautions missionaries to be sensitive to the indigenous church leaders, recognizing that they are important partners in the global work of the church: "Our unique opportunities right now are to see God working through this diversity and not try to control it."[18] Thus, it is essential that the EdSTMer, as all STMers, must be properly prepared vis-à-vis whatever cultural anomalies may exist in the receptor culture.[19]

These, and other cautions, are valid and worthy of serious consideration by prospective EdSTM team leaders as they seek to identify potential local pastors with whom to work in the determined field of service. Having this framework in mind, then, the local church is prepared to initiate and develop a relationship with an indigenous pastor who will serve as liaison and, to some extent, host of the EdSTM.

How can a team find the indigenous pastor with whom they are to work? The 'big picture' answer, of course, is that God will direct them to the right person, in keeping with his call to the church to reach a particular area. The church, however, must play an active role in this process, as well! Thankfully, there are a number of avenues by which the church can initiate contact with pastors in

18. Creson, "Global Perspective," 188.
19. This is discussed in some detail below, under Step 6.

Developing an EdSTM Ministry in the Local Church

the targeted field of service. Among these is the *Missions Handbook*, which lists virtually every missions agency in the United States and Canada according to the nation where they serve. Even though the church is not necessarily intending to align with one or more of these agencies,[20] the agencies can direct the church to either their missionary in that field or to indigenous pastors in that field. This creates opportunities to begin to interact with someone directly connected to the targeted field of service. It may require contacting several agencies at work in a particular area before a potential candidate emerges. Or, this avenue may, in fact, lead nowhere. Still, there are other approaches. In the modern era, virtually anything can be found on the Internet if sufficient effort is employed. This may also prove to be a helpful tool in meeting indigenous pastors. There are doubtlessly websites frequented—and perhaps even hosted—by indigenous pastors. Diligence may well be the only cost associated with finding such pastors.

Finally, despite the era of technology, there is really no equivalent to word of mouth. Quite simply, people know people. It is an amusing parlor game to try to determine how many "degrees" or relationships it takes to connect one person with another person, such as connecting one movie star to another (with whom the first has never worked) by tracing costars who worked with costars, etc. A similar principle undergirds the professional "social" website, *LinkedIn*. On this site, people "connect" with people they know and are then encouraged to "connect" with people whom the people they know, know. The same concept can be employed for a church to find a pastor with whom to work. Begin by asking people in the church to ask people they know about contacts in the field. If that exercise proves fruitless, ask them to ask the people they know to ask people *they* know, and so on. While seeming to be a mind-bending challenge, this process can actually serve to engage the whole local church body in the prospective EdSTM. In the end, as with the raising of funds, the matter must finally rest

---

20. Though partnerships can certainly be cultivated and are often quite helpful.

on the conviction that God will direct the paths of those who are earnestly seeking to serve him.

Step 5: Assembling the Team

At this stage (if not sooner), it is time to begin seriously considering who will constitute the team. The team leaders have already been identified as the missions director and the discipleship director (or their equivalents); however, the most critical appointment for the team will be the person(s) sent to the field. This is where EdSTM diverges from traditional missions models. Typical church-based missions, which rely on non-professional volunteers, send those volunteers into the field to do manual labor, to engage in relational evangelism, or to conduct other indirect forms of missions; rare indeed is the church that sends its non-professional missionaries into the field to instruct indigenous pastors.

With EdSTM, however, that is precisely the model. For this model both recognizes and encourages the gifts and skills of many in the local, American church to *teach*. In others words, there are those who are gifted and skilled sufficiently to teach other adults in the local church; why, then, are these teachers inadequate to teach adults in other countries? The adults in the Majority World are not more likely to possess advanced Bible knowledge or a superior grasp of doctrine relative to those teaching adult Sunday School classes in Minnesota or New Mexico or South Carolina; in fact, the opposite is most often the case. Quite simply, the individual raised in a godly home and/or evangelical church in America, who then studies and prepares to teach other adults, will often have more knowledge about the essentials of the faith—simply by virtue of relentless exposure—than his counterpart in Nicaragua, Pakistan, or Ghana.

This is not, of course, to say that the average American believer is more mature spiritually than the believer in the Majority World; sadly, despite the presence of the proverbial church on every street corner and ready access to instruction in the truths of God, the American church is, to no small degree, spiritually anemic. Nonetheless, those who have taken the time and effort to prepare to teach others in the local church in the West have, at their fingertips, an immeasurable store of resources from which to draw; the pastor or teacher in the Majority World often has nothing more than his Bible, and often even that is not available in his native tongue. Thus, the American AD teacher (assuming he has been placed in that role by virtue of gifts and calling) already has two key ingredients for successful EdSTM: a adequate grasp of a particular biblical or theological theme, and the corresponding gift that enables him to communicate it.

While it can be argued, then, that the typical AD teacher in the United States has the knowledge required for EdSTM, and the communication skills to share that knowledge, this does not mean that every teacher is a candidate for foreign ministry, even EdSTM. Setting aside the obvious potential for disqualification because of serious health issues or responsibilities that preclude time away from home, the fact remains: missions requires a calling from God. Granted, all Christians are, by nature of their calling to salvation, compelled to be witnesses for Christ wherever they may be. Further, as constituent parts of the body of Christ commanded to pray earnestly for workers in the harvest, all Christians are to be in some way involved in missions: either going themselves, or sending with prayer and financial support. That, however, is not the same as saying that every Christian *is* a missionary. Hoke and Taylor share the same conviction, writing:

> We are convinced that *missionary* is not simply a generic term for all Christians doing everything the church does in service to the kingdom of God. We do a disservice to the term by universalizing its use, oversimplifying a rich vocabulary and theology of gifting and vocation . . . Both of us are committed to a robust biblical *theology of vocations* . . . ; a *theology of gifts* . . . ; and a *theology of callings* . . .[21]

---

21. Hoke and Taylor, *Global Mission Handbook*, 22–23; emphasis in original.

While the calling of a STMer or a EdSTMer may not have the same vocational force as the calling of a career missionary, there must be a gifting to serve the kingdom in this way ("not all are apostles," etc.; 1 Cor 12:29). To say that everyone is a teacher or everyone is a missionary essentially distills to *no one* being a teacher and *no one* being a missionary. For the term and the role to have any substance, there must be a corresponding gifting that enables the fulfillment of that calling and, furthermore, the call must be recognizable; that is, both the person (internal testimony) and his sending church (external testimony) must be confident in, and at peace with, the interpretation of the call. Stevens writes,

> There are many reasons a person may apply for a short or long term missionary position, but not all of them are positive or healthy. Questions should be asked regarding the motive for serving, how they see themselves in relation to the work and other people on the field, and if they can commit to the pre-field training that needs to occur.[22]

It is only when these difficult questions have been asked and answered satisfactorily that the mission can proceed, with all involved truly convinced that this person is *God's* person for this work.

Where the non-professional missionary from the West *is* at a seeming disadvantage is in his lack of cultural acclimation vis-à-vis the field of service. However, this apparent obstacle dissolves significantly in light of two principles in the EdSTM model: first, the target is not the unbeliever in the field who is hostile to the gospel and challenging its every expression, but the indigenous pastor who already has embraced the essence of that gospel and, in fact, hungers to understand its beauty more fully. Second, the EdSTM model anticipates the reality of the cultural disconnect and, while not able to remove it entirely, does concentrate on at least rudimentary preparations consistent with the time to be spent in the field with *friends*: or, likeminded followers of Christ. In short, OM

---

22. Stevens, "Recruitment and Training," 28.

has a good yardstick for gauging prospective missionaries: "they need to be *FAT* people: flexible, adaptable, and teachable."[23] The same could be said of any ministry, and EdSTM is certainly no exception. Candidates who meet these qualifications, and are also spiritually mature, will prove to be very useful tools in the able hands of the Master.

Step 6: Training in Content and Culture

It can be said, then, that the prospective EdSTMer has two principle foci upon which to concentrate: the *content* of the workshop he will be leading and the *culture* in which he will be leading it. The former will be more familiar to him, of course; the latter likely considerably less so. However, both are indispensible components of EdSTM and, therefore, require proper preparations. Further, each has its own challenges and cautions, which will now be considered in turn.

Content

Kane rightly noted, "It is imperative that today's missionary have an adequate grasp of Christian theology . . ."[24] Blue is even more emphatic:

> Never in the history of the church has there existed a greater demand for missionaries who are well trained in the Bible and theology. The day when a simplistic approach to missions was acceptable—if, indeed this ever was the case—no longer exists.[25]

Especially in EdSTM, it is critical that the participants will have sufficient grasp of the topic of instruction to teach the indigenous pastor adequately. This is, after all, the very basis of the ministry: indigenous pastors, with an inadequate grasp of Christian

---

23. Tarantal, "Global Perspectives," 252.
24. Kane, *Christian Missions*, 85.
25. Blue, "Theological Training," 177.

doctrine need to have that inadequacy rectified. That being said, there is no reason that an EdSTMer need have a firm grasp on *all* Christian theology. In other words, the very nature of the EdSTM model is to provide lay trainers in a *specific* subject, and it is in this specific subject that the missionary must himself be properly trained. Thus, an EdSTMer serving in the field and conducting a workshop on *Knowing God* would need to have an "adequate grasp" on the doctrines related to the character and attributes of God. It would be less important for this missionary—at least in the context of this workshop—to have as firm a grasp of the doctrines related to eschatology, and less important still to be able to articulate a defined ecclesiology. Each workshop, then, would require only that the missionary become sufficiently prepared to discuss the general themes and perspectives related to the subject matter at hand, much as the AD teacher need only be proficient in the subject of his AD class.

One method of training potential EdSTM participants is by means of church-based, intensive programs that essentially mirror the training workshop which the EdSTMer will lead in the field. Adhering to the biblical principle of discipleship that it is not enough to *teach* the indigenous pastors but that they must also be *taught to teach* (2 Tim 2:2), the initial EdSTM workshop should not only teach the EdSTMer in the relevant subject matter, but prepare him to teach it, as well. To this end, workbooks are employed, in addition to lectures and secondary materials, which provide the students with everything necessary to conduct a similar class in their church, their community, or in the missions field as EdSTM.

Finally, however, it is not necessary for the EdSTMer to be an *expert* even in the subject matter of the workshop; many of the potential EdSTMers in the American church are already considerably more advanced in their understanding of the Christian faith than the indigenous pastors with whom they will be working and, therefore, they need only a concentrated period of guided study to be adequately prepared to conduct the workshop. It is important to emphasize, however, that a faulty or errant theological framework, as least as it pertains to the essentials of the faith, would be a significant hindrance to the success of EdSTM; in fact, it is the very prevalence of such bad theology that EdSTM is designed to correct.

Culture

In addition to proper preparation in the context of the EdSTM, the prospective participant(s) must also become prepared to enter into and interact with a culture different than their own: sometimes, radically different. The importance of this preparation may be demonstrated both negatively and positively. First, poor cultural preparation may (and likely will) lead to poor results. Quite simply, there must be a point of connection *other than the common faith* between the EdSTMer and the host pastor(s). While that bond of faith will surely extend the working relationship considerably farther than would be possible if it were absent, the faith, in and of itself, does not facilitate *communication*. In other words, a Christian from Indonesia and a Christian from Tanzania may hold a significant breadth of common beliefs and convictions, yet be unable to discuss them in any meaningful way without the connecting bridges of language and culture. This is why the EdSTM must take the necessary steps to alleviate this barrier as much as possible.

The first consideration in any foreign missions enterprise is the barrier of language; this is no different for EdSTM. There must be an avenue to convey and receive information. Typically, due to the intentional brevity of the mission, the EdSTM would not set out to learn the language of the receptor culture. Therefore, there are two remaining options: 1) work with a host pastor who speaks English (assuming that to be the language of the EdSTMer), or 2) engage an interpreter. Either option can work; however, this would need to be addressed at the outset (in step 4, above, for example).

The next consideration would be the broader context of culture, generally. This includes language, of course, but it also includes such variables as customs, traditions, and rituals in all manner of interpersonal relationships. Is the receptor culture individualistic, like America? Probably not. Far more common are tribal, clan, or at least family networks. Is punctuality of prime importance? Often not. It is not uncommon for people in the Majority World to view appointments merely as *suggestions*. Is the receptor culture more naturally drawn to goals/ends or to processes/means? Sometimes the answers are obvious; other times, they are more nuanced. In any event, investing some time researching such things will go a long way toward reducing (if perhaps not eliminating) cultural clashes that can result in confusion or hurt feelings, both of which impede the effectiveness of the mission in the time-sensitive format of EdSTM.

Positively, cultural preparation can be a great benefit to both the EdSTM and the host pastor(s). Referring to the two-tiered approach to cultural adaptation provided by Duane Elmer,[26] Donna Sheets points out that most missionaries come to the question of culture with one of two "tracks," which she defines as, "the upper track, which begins with an approach of openness, acceptance, and trust, and the lower track, which begins with an approach of fear, suspicion, and inflexibility."[27] Taking the "upper track" can lead to far greater depth of interaction, a more fulfilling missions encounter, and, ultimately, greater success in the goal of advancing the kingdom of God. It has been noted that "the cross-cultural short-term experience develops world Christians as it allows the team members to see another culture as it really is—allowing God to experientially teach them more about himself and the infinite variety of His working in various cultures."[28] Thus, while a prevailing critique of STM is valid (i.e., that the trips often reflect more in the lives of the STMers than in those in the field), this is not necessarily a bad thing. In EdSTM, for instance, a properly prepared participant can be equipped to have a lasting and positive effect in the field of service, while at the same time, experiencing significant spiritual growth as a result of the cultural exposure.

26. Elmer, *Connections*, 72–73.
27. Sheets, "Mission Trip Training Program," 47.
28. Ibid., 43.

Developing an EdSTM Ministry in the Local Church

Not only is cultural preparation beneficial to the EdSTMer, however; it is also helpful for those in the receptor culture. As Stevens writes, "Cultural understanding prepares better witnesses for Christ. It is the opposite of the 'ugly American' who travels for his own pleasure and benefit with no regard for the places and people he visits."[29] To whatever degree the perception of the "ugly American" can be minimized, the focus can be redirected to the task at hand: training pastors and church leaders to be better equipped to lead those providentially placed under their spiritual care. In the end, however, it is wise to consider Anthony's summary of the matter:

> No amount of preparation and advanced orientation can eliminate all problems or obstacles. Some things are bound to go wrong even after the most detailed plans have been developed. However, the more forethought you give to preparation and training before you depart for your short-term trip, the better off you and your group will be before you arrive.[30]

Potential participants in EdSTM (or any missions work, really) should not be paralyzed by the reality that things will inevitably go wrong on some level. Conversely, they should also not be lulled into believing that *nothing* will go wrong and, consequently, be little concerned with investing the time and energy into preparation. An adequate training program, increasingly improved over time as it is implemented and modified in response to experiences or unforeseen challenges, can in fact provide a sure foundation and an effective launching pad for EdSTMers. The team leaders need only insure that adequate attention is given in such a program to both *context* and *culture*; in so doing, they can trust that the most prohibitive obstacles have been removed.

---

29. Stevens, "Recruitment and Training," 28.
30. Anthony, *Missions Boom*, 124–25.

Step 7: Fundraising

EdSTM, like every missions model and, in fact, like every ministry, requires funding. A church that has enthusiastically embraced the EdSTM model, particularly among its leadership, may be inclined to simply write the associated costs into the church's annual budget; however, this may have inadvertent consequences. For instance, church members may be deprived of the joy of "co-laboring" in the work, and, for the EdSTMer, the blessing of fundraising could be lost; for indeed, "raising funds may be hard on the flesh but it is good for the spirit."[31] In a particularly illustrative way, Kane describes this potential blessing:

> When the [missionary] first starts out he is filled with fear and trepidation. How will he ever be able to raise that huge amount of money? It seems like an impossible task. In his dilemma he is cast on the Lord in a new way
> . . .
> As the funds come in, sometimes from the most unexpected sources he rejoices in the goodness of God . . . By the time the last dollar is in he is ready to sing the doxology. He is the happiest person in the world. God has provided above that he dared expect. He will never be the same again.[32]

In fact, a prospective EdSTMer that is a) not this committed to the task, or b) not this thrilled by God confirming his call to the field by resourcing the trip, may well *not* be called by God to serve in this way or at this time. An EdSTMer, just as any other missionary, must be convinced that the work is the right thing for him to do; he must want to do it (because of a desire to serve the Lord—not because of a desire for adventure!); and he must be wholly invested in the work. This last point requires his time and study in preparation, of course, but also would include time in prayer, entreating God to provide for the attendant needs, as well as time spent with other believers, sharing his excitement, passion,

---

31. Kane, *Life and Work*, 71.
32. Ibid.

and motivation. The EdSTMer must, in other words, long to serve a particular people in a particular place at a particular time.

A wide-reaching misperception in the realm of missions fundraising is the real challenge some—particularly Americans—have when it comes to the (perceived) embarrassment of asking for money. Many missions trips are never realized because the person who believes in the mission is not as convinced of the ancillary work of fundraising. Stevens succinctly sums up the matter in light of this common perspective on finances and missions: "The self-sufficient attitude of 'I'll go when I can afford it' is respectable in our culture but not necessarily pleasing to God."[33] The prospective missionary must be encouraged by the team leaders to develop a healthy philosophy of fundraising that sees this vital work as a blessing—both for the one raising the funds and the ones who are given the opportunity to give. Anything less will have the net result of either an unfunded (and thus likely unrealized) missions project; an underfunded missions project that misses its objective; or a self-funded (or church-funded) missions project, which sends out a missionary who has not adequately incorporated the broader Body of Christ in his mission.

Still, it is not unreasonable for the sending church to be among the missionary's primary supporters. After all, the local church represents a *collective* interest of members of the Body and (hopefully!) a portion of regular tithes and/or offerings are earmarked for missions, generally. Thus, it is appropriate that, after much prayer and counsel, the team (or those responsible for the allocation of the church's missions budget) consider how the church may show support for the EdSTM. In order to not circumvent the central role in individuals supporting the missions work, the church should perhaps offer to supply the *last* half of the necessary funds (after the first half has been raised) or to offer a matching gift that likewise serves to encourage the EdSTMer to raise support outside of the comfort of the team that is sending him.

There are several resources available to assist the potential missionary in raising financial support. Perhaps one of the most

---

33. Stevens, "Recruitment and Training," 26.

comprehensive of these is Scott Morton's well-received work, *Funding Your Ministry: An In-Depth, Biblical Guide for Successfully Raising Personal Support*. In this book, Morton addresses virtually every aspect of fundraising, including the perspective missionary's "attitude," specific fundraising strategies (from both individual donors and churches), common mistakes, and "myths" that often cause potential missionaries to approach fundraising in the wrong way. At the heart of Morton's book, and the impetus for it, is his belief that inadequate support is a critical problem in the missions ministry of the church. He writes that this problem "contributes heavily to marital discord, personal stress, and ill-advised ministry strategy."[34] To avoid such crises, Morton hopes to point potential missionaries toward the path of successfully funded ministry, believing rightly that "God is the source [of support]—not our donors, not our plans, not our hard work."[35] By correctly focusing on the provision of the Lord, the EdSTMer will be able to agree with the classic maxim uttered by missionary pioneer, Hudson Taylor: "God's work, done God's way, will never lack God's supply."[36] In fact, the history of Christian missions should provide the confidence that the modern EdSTMer must possess to flame his own passion for ministry that others are compelled to join with him in it: God has always met the needs of those who were sold out to serving him, in his way and in his timing. It has been said that "Prayer is the real work of the ministry. Service is just gathering in the results of prayer."[37] Hoke and Taylor go on to encourage prospective missionaries, "Bathe yourself and your donors in prayer before, during and after [the] fundraising journey. God will go before you."[38] In ministry generally, and in the critical field of missions particularly, can a true believer in Christ really doubt that God's promises are unshakably true? As Paul wrote, with such

---

34. Morton, *Funding Your Ministry*, xi.
35. Ibid., 13.
36. Lyall, *Passion*, 37.
37. Hoke and Taylor, *Global Mission Handbook*. 144.
38. Ibid.

assurance, "My God shall supply all your needs, according to his riches in glory by Christ Jesus" (Phil 4:19).

Step 8: Deployment

After the field has been determined and the EdSTMer has been thoroughly prepared, and after the funds have been raised, the time has come to send him into that field. This is a critical stage in the process, concerned with the logistics of deployment. This includes such mundane issues as vaccinations, visas, travel insurance, and itineraries; it also includes the more weighty issues of organizing prayer in the face of spiritual and physical danger; the sending church actually, formally and corporately, *sending* the EdSTMer into the field; and so forth. For the EdSTMer, there are some often overlooked details that can produce stress while in the field. For instance, who will collect the EdSTMer's mail if he is leaving behind an empty home while on the field? What about bills that will come due during his absence? These and other considerations, which are so much part and parcel of daily life that they are seldom discussed, must be addressed.

Missions agencies usually have extensive knowledge in the logistics of travel: the safest airlines, the most economical times for travel, the visa requirements of each country. The church-based EdSTM will be less likely to have such encyclopedic knowledge. Therefore, this area will require dedicated research. Internet searches will reveal many websites that discuss the merits of these travel issues.[39] A simple investment of time can reap a reward of cheaper airfares and (relatively) stress-free passage through international airports, as well as safe and (relatively) clean accommodations in the field. It is critical that such research be retained and catalogued in some way, so as to allow for access later, thereby reducing the research time for subsequent trips.

---

39. At the time of this writing, some of the sites I have used are: kayak.com for airfare rates; hotels.com and agoda.com for hotels; airlinequality.com for rankings and reviews of airlines; and tripadvisor.com for reviews of airlines, hotels, and even restaurants, written by other travelers.

Step 6 above considered the theoretical interaction with culture; here that interaction becomes tangible. The EdSTMer will quickly be confronted with the need for such simple but profound adaptations as a lack of flush toilets (or, in extreme cases, *any* toilets), non-potable water, and sporadic electrical services. Communicating with home may be severely restricted, as many fields of service have only intermittent Internet service, if at all, and telephone calls to/from some Majority World countries are prohibitively expensive and should probably be avoided, save in the case of emergencies.

Regardless of the degree of preparation, however, the EdSTMer must be prepared to be flexible. Nah suggests that, while there are considerable resources for pre-field preparation and post-field debriefing, there is less information for on-field ministry. He notes that this may be because "it is with the assumption that sufficient pre-field preparation renders on-field instructions as extemporaneous." He cautions, however, that while pre-field training can anticipate a great many issues, "others are impossible to plan for," because "STM trips are notorious for attracting non-contingent diversions."[40] Granted, many STMers have on-field problems due to a lack of preparation, such as the young lady who went into the mission field thinking that the American embassy would be picking her up from the airport![41] Still, while the astute EdSTMer will carefully take advantage of whatever cultural preparations are available, he must also acknowledge that there will inevitably be situations that fall outside of any preparations. Plenty of patience and prayer will go a long way toward extricating the EdSTMer from unforeseen cultural challenges.

Once the EdSTMer has arrived at the prearranged teaching location (often the indigenous church, or a meeting room in the EdSTMer's hotel), it is time to get to the heart of the ministry: teaching pastors. Presumably, the EdSTMer already has basic teaching skills (as an AD teacher), is already familiar with the host/liaison pastor (with whom the team leaders—as well as the

---

40. Nah, "Paradigms," 68.
41. Pirolo, "Raising the Standard," 172.

EdSTMer himself—ought to have been in contact for some time), and is adequately prepared in both the content of the lesson materials and the cultural context in which he will be teaching. Using the materials developed in step 2 above, the EdSTMer will now begin to progress through the workbook. He will begin each section by explaining the doctrine it contains, and will read the associated verses from the Bible. He will then begin to explain the doctrine simply, yet accurately.

This is the important first step in the teaching process: make sure that the pastors with whom the EdSTMer is working are themselves grasping the essence of the doctrine. The EdSTMer should allow ample time for discussions and questions, and should be prepared to stay on a particular subject until he is convinced that his students really do understand the doctrine, and understand it in its orthodox formulation. Then—and only then—is it appropriate for him to move on to the interactive element of the workbook: the cooperative effort of turning the workbook into a teaching tool for the indigenous church.

At this point in each chapter or section (which should be restricted to only one doctrine or biblical focus or theme), the EdSTMer and the local pastors will begin to craft illustrations that they (the pastors) believe will aid in the comprehension of the doctrine by their people. It is critical at this point that the EdSTMer see his role only as that of *doctrinal mediator*, ensuring that the essence of the doctrine is faithfully preserved. In other words, the cultural framework in which that doctrine is illustrated is the bailiwick of the indigenous pastors—and *not* of the EdSTMer. This is precisely where so many STMs fall short, and it is precisely why EdSTM was conceived in the form presented in this study: no outsider ever understands a culture as fluently as an insider. Therefore, in matters of context and integrating the truth of the doctrine into the receptor culture, the indigenous pastors are indispensable.

Finally, the EdSTMer will encourage the pastors to craft response questions that they believe would be helpful in their own teaching; that is, questions that they (as teachers) would ask their students/churches in order to insure that they (the students) also properly comprehend the underlying doctrine. These questions should:

1. Be open-ended (i.e., not simply requiring "yes" or "no" responses);
2. Incorporate the doctrine; and
3. Reflect the cultural illustration(s)

All the while, the EdSTMer is making careful notes of what the pastors are saying—even of *how* they are saying it (to remain faithful to their intent), in both the illustrations and response questions. These additions will be incorporated into the workbook after the EdSTMer returns home, and finalized copies will be delivered to the indigenous pastors to use in their churches.

Any cross-cultural academic work can be challenging; if such work is conducted via an interpreter, it can be exhausting. Consequently, the EdSTMer should insure that the group takes sufficient breaks (tea breaks, while less common to Americans, are rather expected in much of the world). Also, reasonable classroom hours should be established that take into consideration:

1. The pastors' transit times (often they will be arriving on foot or by circuitous public transport systems);
2. Their pastoral obligations (e.g., if they have midweek services, weddings, funerals, or other such obligations);
3. Their family obligations (often these pastors will also have household responsibilities, such as farming, etc.);
4. Their spiritual wellbeing (as with all believers, the pastors will need to have daily time alone with the Lord); and
5. Their preparations for each day's class (time to process and reflect at the end of the day should be included in the daily schedule)

In all, a typical EdSTM will consist of five full days of instruction (roughly 30 hours of actual classroom time is ideal); often, the EdSTMer can arrive a day or two early (or stay a day or two afterward) and enjoy the singular blessing of worshiping with the indigenous church. The EdSTMer must also allow adequate time for his own rest and spiritual nourishment while in the field, outside of the times spent with the pastors. This is often neglected by STMers, as they see the whole of their ministry as time with God. However, there is no substitute for private, quiet times with the Lord, even in the midst of hectic missions trips.

The EdSTMer will, of course, be eager to capture pictures and video of the whole experience. This is good to do; however, care must be taken to respect cultural practices (some cultures are opposed to having their pictures taken because of superstitious beliefs) and even local laws (in Burma, for instance, taking pictures of any military or government building is grounds for imprisonment!). Also, it is important that the EdSTMer focus his camera on what really matters: the people. The pictures serve two primary purposes: the EdSTMer's own memories, and his stories, which he will share after returning home. Pictures of lions and ancient pyramids and strange cuisine may stir up the hearts of adventurers; pictures of brothers and sisters in Christ in strange lands, with their children, their Bibles, and their smiles, will stir up the hearts of missionaries.

Step 9: Debriefing

Jennifer Collins points out that a failure to debrief STMers is a critical failing in the evangelical church. "Following a short-term experience, participants are sometimes thrust back into their home culture and responsibilities without any assistance in processing their missions encounter. This inattention leaves them bewildered and feeling alone." She goes on to conclude that the net effect of not being properly debriefed and guided through the process of evaluating the experience may be that the STMers "mentally file away the experience, thereby reducing its overall impact."[42] Another writer refers to the missionary's reentry as "reverse culture

---

42. Collins, "Short-Term Missions," 318.

shock," as they are "unsettled by the values they see in their own nation."[43] While it may seem as if this would only be a concern for returning LTMers, even a brief stay in a wholly other culture can create a lasting imprint that forever alters the way in which one's own culture is viewed. Seeing children with missing limbs, ravaged by disease, malnourished, and begging for food to survive another day will break even the most callous heart. As those called by God in Christ, missionaries have had their stony hearts replaced with tender "hearts of flesh" (Ezek 36:26), and are even more susceptible to the impact such experiences deliver. Coming home to see children, about the same age, eating well, laughing, and enjoying the bountiful blessings to be had in America is, indeed, a harsh contrast. Returning EdSTMers must be guided through this reintroduction into their own culture in such a way as to not be ashamed of the blessings God has poured out upon the West, yet not to take such blessings for granted, either. A proper balance can provide the returning EdSTMer with a healthy, fresh amazement in the face of God's unmerited favor.

Not just the returning EdSTMer is in view at this stage; the church to which he returns is front and center, as well. All returning missionaries—whether STMers or LTMers—have the opportunity to describe the work of God in foreign lands, the movement of the Holy Spirit among the churches there, and the joys of watching a new believer being baptized or a new church being planted. In this regard, the returning EdSTMer is no different; he has a story to tell. Pictures and videos make the "alien" culture come alive to those in the pews in American churches. While it may be true that a picture says a thousand words, it is important, that those words are not the only ones the church hears! The returning EdSTM must engage the people, must stimulate their passion for the world and for the Gospel, and must take the time to introduce the people on the screen to the people in the pews. Michael Jaffarin describes this process as "instilling a missional vision in every member."[44] Ron Blue offers some helpful tips to returning STMers to facilitate

---

43. Pirolo, "Raising the Standard," 173.
44. Jaffarin, "Good News and Bad News," 178.

Developing an EdSTM Ministry in the Local Church

this vision.[45] First, he suggests that returning STMers always be ready to share an experience from the mission field in a "crisp one minute story." He also suggests that the STMer actively look for opportunities to share these stories, perhaps in small group contexts, and to use word pictures and illustrations. It is important that the STMer tell his stories in ways that are gripping yet not embellished. The aim is to get the listener to a place where they see the EdSTMer's vision and claim it as their own, as well. In this way, the vitally important ongoing nature of EdSTM can be realized in the local church. The goal, after all, is not simply to make the indigenous pastors smarter, but to encourage the perpetuation of discipleship—in their churches, and in the EdSTMer's sending church, as well.

Step 10: Replication

If it really is the desire of the local church to begin an ongoing ministry of EdSTM (as opposed to a one-off event), the returning EdSTMer is in a unique position to serve in enlisting future candidates. From this position of experience, he is able to paint a realistic picture of what this ministry actually entails. The team leaders must be aware of this potential role, and employ it wherever feasible to maintain the church's excitement for the ministry.

One way this can be done is to encourage returning EdSTMers to serve in the church as AD teachers; in fact, in this model, the typical EdSTMer would already be accustomed to this role. The subject matter of their AD classes, however, could take on a different *flavor*, which reflects both the content of the subject they taught in the EdSTM and the context (i.e., culture) in which they taught it. Other prospective EdSTMers should be encouraged to attend these classes, be active participants in discussions, and prayerfully seek to discern if an internal calling to a similar ministry exists for them, as well, because one missionary's "experience can be a great magnet for others, convincing them of the

---

45. Blue, "Tell the Story," 111.

need to become world Christians."[46] After all, this idea of being "world Christians" is really nothing more than being fully engaged in one's relationship with Jesus. This does not always require that a Christian participate personally in foreign missions as a "goer," of course, but it *does* require that a Christian be passionate about the expansion of the kingdom of Christ in the world through the carrying out of the Great Commission—perhaps as a "sender." Either way, the returning EdSTMer can wield considerable influence in helping the members of the local church to develop a meaningful and lifelong appreciation for the global church. Some may well sense, through the words and images of the returning EdSTMer, that the Lord would have them go; others may be convicted of the need for greater commitment to prayer and financial support of those who go. Still others may not yet know what God would have them to do, but this may be the time for serious reflection and self-examination.

The returning EdSTMer may be a Barnabas to a budding Paul; or, he may be the Paul—turning the EdSTM experience into a springboard for vocational missions. In either case, the EdSTMer should ask himself: "Who is your Timothy?" Perhaps the team leaders should ask him this, as well. The point of this exercise is to exhort the returning EdSTMer to see the long vision of ministry, to commit to continuing his labors for the Lord well after he returns from the field. In other words, whom can he mentor? Mentoring is simply "a relational experience where one person is empowered by another through the sharing of God-given resources."[47] God has given the EdSTMer a bevy of resources to share: cultural awareness (including, perhaps, lessons learned the hard way), teaching and communication skills (at home and abroad), and the interpersonal experience that is fostered in an EdSTM environment. These are not "talents" to be buried, but are to be "invested" (cf. Matt 25:14-30). They should be poured into the lives of others, in the prayerful hope that another person may be blessed to serve.

---

46. Hoke, "Missionary Training," 217.
47. Stanley and Clinton, *Connecting*, 33.

Finally, the goal of replication is not only to be an exchange from one person to another, but also from one place to another or from one time to another. In other words, the returning EdSTMer should not consider his work in missions to be completed, simply because he has finished a particular assignment. On the contrary, he should be encouraged by the team leaders to consider redeploying to other fields of service where similar needs exist. As an EdSTMer becomes increasingly familiar with a particular subject, his effectiveness is likewise bound to increase in the field. As he seeks out creative ways to communicate truth in the field, the learning curve is accelerated with each subsequent communication. Therefore, he may excel in communicating the same material in another location. On the other hand, the returning EdSTMer is also now at least somewhat familiar with the culture where he served. He may also have formed relationships that were particularly meaningful and he may wish to nurture these relationships further. Therefore, he may prefer to consider returning to the same field of service to teach a different subject. In either case, the EdSTMer is building upon his strengths: either in a particular subject in multiple fields, or in a particular field with multiple subjects.

Anticipating Objections

Having outlined a plan for implementing EdSTM as a ministry of the local church, a number of potential objections may be anticipated. Some objections to STM, generally, are addressed elsewhere in this study. Other objections can be distilled under three broad themes: the senders (the church); the sent (the EdSTMer); and the field in which the EdSTM is carried out (the targeted field of service).

> *Objection: The church is an inadequate missions sending agency; i.e., the era of missionaries who are solely church-based has been eclipsed by "professional" sending agencies.*

For much of the modern era, Protestant missions have increasingly been a work overseen and carried out through missions agencies. Local churches would send new missionaries out, of course, but they would really be sending them to an agency rather than to the field, as it was the agency that then assumed oversight. It has been argued that this arrangement "seems to cause a relational breakdown between missionary and church, with the church feeling like they are only a payer of services rendered."[48] Whether this is so or not likely varies as churches do; however, it is true that some churches are reestablishing themselves as senders in more than just financial terms: taking on the responsibilities of the physical and spiritual well-being of the missionary, as well as monitoring his ministry in the field.[49] This may seem like a weighty responsibility in the modern missions environment; however, it is arguably as old as the New Testament church, where Paul and Barnabas were sent out by the church in Antioch to whom they reported back about their ministry (Acts 13:1–3; cf. 14:21–28). To be sure, this level of commitment would be foreign to many local churches, and the church's team would have to serve as a de facto agency. Still, this role is consistent with the church's role, in general:

> The community of faith, the backbone and model of truth, lives to take the gospel to all nations, until the end of times and to the end of the earth. That endeavor is the main character in missions. To carry out the *Missio Dei*, we must start from the local church (*Missio Ecclesiae*).[50]

It is my conviction that the Church should send missionaries and that those missionaries should be accountable *primarily* to the sending church (and not, for instance, to an independent mission agency). There are certainly legitimate roles for sodalities in demonstrating the love of Christ to the world (e.g., Compassion International, Samaritan's Purse, etc.). And, of course, such groups will share the gospel as the situations warrant during their missions of mercy. However, insofar as groups are established *specifically for*

---

48. Stairs, "Global Approach," 72.

49. Stairs writes, "[T]here seems to be a trend in North American churches towards full and active partnership between church and missionary. (Ibid.)

50. Bahamonde "Contextualization," 230.

Developing an EdSTM Ministry in the Local Church

the purpose of sending missionaries, they need to be under the leadership of the local church. This can be accomplished through a local church directly or, alternatively, through a denominational mission agency that is itself under such leadership.

An integral aspect of any missions endeavor should be to encourage the new convert to become intimately affiliated with a local, biblically-sound church. The church is central to the *Missio Dei*. Rather than fracturing and creating multiple entities, the most biblical idea is for the church to grow, all the while retaining submission to spiritual authorities in the local church.

> *Objection: Proposed participants (i.e., lay volunteers) are not formally trained to teach pastors, and are thus not suited for the work of educational missions.*

It has been established above that the model of EdSTM proposed herein:

1. Acknowledges the need for missionaries to be properly equipped [in the subject(s) they will be teaching];
2. Assumes that AD teachers in the local church are often already thus equipped; and
3. Argues that it is the role of the EdSTM team leaders to insure that the prospective candidate is, in fact, adequately prepared to teach the subject under consideration.

I established a training center in our local church specifically for the purposes of training prospective teachers and missionaries throughout the community in Bible and doctrine.[51] Similar models could be instituted in any local church to provide the necessary training and resource development associated with an effective EdSTM ministry.

> *Objection: The receptor country will not be prepared to function as host for the EdSTM (i.e., concerns about logistics; selecting in-country participants and excluding*

---

51. See www.capefearschool.org.

others; and overseeing implementation of post-EdSTM discipleship programs).

Simply because such practices are foreign to some cultures, it may be that the indigenous host pastor may not be skilled in such logistics as scheduling workshops, procuring supplies (e.g., pens, paper, etc.), or arranging meals for workshop participants. The EdSTMer can offer to help with such matters, although it is also important that the EdSTMer not seek to superimpose foreign methodology over existing cultural expectations. For instance, the EdSTM venue will probably look quite different from a typical American office conference room or even the educational wing of an American church. That, in and of itself, is not a *problem* to be *fixed*. Functionality over form should be the guiding principle. However, the EdSTMer can certainly assist the host pastor, particularly in regard to handling whatever financial arrangements may arise (for meals, meeting rooms, etc.) as these are often issues that cause great consternation to the indigenous pastor who has no financial resources and yet, has a culturally-imposed obligation to be a good host to visitors. The EdSTMer can subtly absolve the host of such cultural niceties.

With regard to selecting the participants for the workshop: if the host pastor does not make that decision, who will? The EdSTMer (presumably) has little to no independent knowledge of the particular details surrounding the need for pastoral education in the field of service; in fact, this is one of the principle contributions that the EdSTM will expect from the host pastor. Still, the EdSTM can assist in this process by establishing some ground rules, such as limiting the group size to five to seven students (this size best facilitates discussions and a working group rather than a lecture format), and asking that the participants be pastors themselves or others tasked with teaching in the local church.

Finally, with regard to the post-workshop implementation of the cooperatively-developed resource material, there is little that the EdSTMer can do to insure it; however, an ancillary benefit of the EdSTM model is that it certainly allows for (and even encourages) the continuing relationship between the EdSTMer and the host pastor, even after the workshop has been concluded. Assuming at least intermittent access to the Internet in the field of service, emails can be exchanged on a regular basis, serving to encourage the indigenous pastor in his ministry (including the proper use of the workbooks), as well as fostering a general sense of deepening fellowship between the EdSTMer and the host pastor. Such an ongoing nurturing of these new relationships can only serve to strengthen both the indigenous church and the American church, as they observe and even participate in the gracious work of God, gathering together his people in the global Body of Christ.

Summary

The objections anticipated above, together with others previously considered, do not invalidate the strength of the model proposed herein. The local church that adopts a ministry of EdSTM and follows the steps outlined in this chapter will be doing a significant service toward the fulfillment of the Great Commission. While these steps may be modified or expanded to meet the particular needs of a particular church, the model as a whole reflects an effective ministry strategy for local churches in America.

5
Conclusion

The Need for Pastoral Education in the Majority World

The purpose of this study is not to suggest that uneducated men cannot be called of God and empowered by the Holy Spirit to do great things; history reveals quite the contrary, as God has demonstrated his desire to work in and through those who are the least in the world's eyes. Lowly shepherds were the first honored to worship the newly incarnate Messiah; and simple fishermen were charged with taking the gospel of Jesus Christ to the ends of the world. Uneducated men have played significant roles in the modern era, as well. D. L. Moody was a simple shoe salesman who ended his formal education in the fifth grade and yet lived a life in ministry that would impact countless people for generations. Likewise, the "Prince of Preachers," Charles Spurgeon, was not seminary-educated, and yet his sermons continue to be used of God to change lives.

Yet for every Moody or Spurgeon, there are countless other Christian pastors—in the Majority World and in the West, as well—whom God has not chosen to equip supernaturally, who lack fundamental training in Bible and theology, and whose ministries reflect the kind of passion that is warned against in the Bible as "zeal without knowledge" (Prov 19:12). As R. Fowler White cautions, the dangers are real, indeed:

Conclusion

A well-meaning but untrained minister might fall into doctrinal error or even heresy and take his congregation with him. The congregation expects the minister to be the 'expert' on the teachings of the biblical text. Thus, the minister's error may have far-reaching implications.[1]

It may be concluded, then, that, in order to minimize the potential "far-reaching implications" of doctrinal error, pastors must be thoroughly equipped to fulfill their calling. It remains true, therefore, that proper training is a good thing; yet this presents a unique problem in the Majority World vis-à-vis contemporary American missions models.

The Inadequacies of the Present Missions Paradigm

This problem has been demonstrated herein; namely, that there is insufficient pastoral education for the global church, and missions—as presently done—does not adequately address this need. From the time of Hudson Taylor's insistence on evangelism as the primary focus in missions to the detriment of discipling a cadre of indigenous leaders who are properly educated in Bible and doctrine,[2] the global church has been decidedly broader than it is deep. While this has the seemingly appealing benefit of enabling the claim of widespread expansion of the Christian faith throughout the world, it poorly reflects the reality that, in many cases, the "Christian faith" that is being propagated is either woefully deficient or, worse, comingled with concepts from other religions, folk superstitions, or cultural traditions to such a degree as to render the resultant faith patently *un*-Christian. The need exists for a revitalized focus on the training of indigenous pastors—and this need is becoming progressively more critical.

Tennent suggests that there has long been a practice in missions of an "overly privatized" approach that produced only an

1. White, "Seminary Education."
2. Cf. Neill, *History,* 283.

"individualistic and minimalistic" response.³ He mentions, anecdotally, that he has observed instances where "discipleship often *precedes* conversion by many years."⁴ In this, he rightly encourages missionaries to engage in dialogic discipleship that interacts with the receptor culture's presuppositions and uniquely-situated worldview. Only then can the gospel be grasped fully enough to support the weight of a profession of faith in Christ. In the present missions paradigm, however, there are simply not enough LTMers to engage in such discipleship with each and every people group around the world, and the bulk of STMers—while they may be doing good—are doing little real discipleship.

There remains a significant gap between 1) the important work that LTM accomplishes in translation, church planting, discipleship, and theological training, among other foci, and 2) the myriad needs in the global church. STM is meeting some of those needs where LTM is not; particularly, in the areas of humanitarian and development projects. What remain most notably unmet are the needs in the global church for theological training. EdSTM seeks to bridge the gap between the present missions paradigm and that need.

As stated at the outset, the danger for many American churches is a complacent acceptance of missions models that, in actuality, do little to fulfill the Great Commission mandate to "make disciples." Sending a monthly support check to one or two LTMers and sending out the occasional team from the youth group to erect a church building is a good start; however, there is much more work to be done, and Christ has ordained that this work be accomplished through his people. No church is excluded from some form of participation.

---

3. Tennent, *Invitation*, 81.
4. Ibid.; emphasis in original.

Conclusion

The Church as Incubator for Educational Short Term Missions

Having determined that the problem does, in fact, exist and having further determined that the present missions models are not adequately addressing that problem, the question persists: What, then, is the solution? The model proposed herein, EdSTM, is certainly one answer. Further, it is a particularly biblical answer, because it recognizes the role of the local church in missions and seeks to employ non-professional missionaries in that capacity. Writing on the relationship between the local church and missions, Peruvian pastor Marcos Bahamonde observed:

> Jesus Christ said, "Therefore go and make disciples of all nations *[ethnes]*. God says to make disciples, not converts. Faithfulness to discipleship deeply seeks the destruction of the structures that harm mission. There is no honor in discipleship if we do not integrate the disciple into the communion of the body of Christ and teach him or her to obey the command holistically. According to the apostle Paul, local congregations served as bridges for their work in, from, and to other cultures of the world with the gospel.[5]

While Bahamonde's immediate context is that typical STMs are *not* adequate to bridge the cultural gap in missions and that this, in turn, necessitates a vigorous indigenous church, his underlying point about the centrality of the local church's role in missions is valid and timely.[6] In fact, elsewhere, he writes: "The local church is an active agent of mission and is the channel through which God develops his work. The community of faith is missionary by nature and serves under the dynamics of the Holy Spirit."[7] Another writer puts it this way: "The main missionary purpose of the existence of

---

5. Bahamonde, "Contextualization," 232–3.

6. In fact, I have argued herein that STM does fail, generally, if the goal is cross-cultural evangelism; where STM (or, rather, EdSTM) succeeds, is when the missionary is working with people in the field who are already Christian (i.e., pastors), and thus less sensitive to cultural offense.

7. Ibid., 245.

the church is to carry on God's mission through Christ on earth."[8] EdSTM is keenly aware of the church's missionary nature and purpose, and I am convinced that purpose extends to every believer in the church. While it is not uncommon for American pastors to occasionally engage in EdSTM, the model proposed herein seeks to integrate non-professional missionaries into the Kingdom's labors, rather than relying wholly upon vocational ministers (such as pastors) to do so. Consequently, the whole of the local church begins to increasingly sense that they share a pivotal role in the growth and maturity of the indigenous church, and that they are encouraged to participate—as goers or senders—in the *koinonia* of the global church.

In fact, because of the lack of LTMers, vocational ministers in the West are not likely to be able to fill the void anyway; they have other duties related to their particular callings (e.g., as pastor), which all too often preclude sustained work in the field. Thus, the needs cannot be met if the only EdSTMers are pastors or seminary professors; the potential pool of available participants is simply too small. On the other hand, many American churches have a wealth of qualified AD teachers, whose biblical/doctrinal knowledge and experience far exceeds that of the typical pastor in the Majority World. Many of these AD teachers also have a heart for missions and a genuine desire to see the Kingdom of God grow throughout the world.

The typical mindset, however, is that the only STM work available (to these AD teachers or any other non-professionals) involves humanitarian and/or social projects. Again, while these may be good works, they often require physical abilities that some of the more seasoned AD teachers cannot do (or simply prefer not to), and so such STMs are less appealing to the heart of the one gifted as a teacher. Granted, these AD teachers—particularly if they also have a heart for missions—may be encouraged to pursue vocational missions ministry. Such a commitment, of course, requires major life changes and long-term commitments (ergo, the dearth of LTMers), and, further, simply because the AD teacher

---

8. Olatoyan, "Local Church," 119.

Conclusion

longs to be involved in missions, does not mean that vocational ministry is his calling. Consequently, in far too many situations throughout the United States, these resources (qualified teachers) are not being utilized efficiently. EdSTM seeks to provide one remedy.

Summary of Benefits in the Educational Short Term Missions Model

EdSTM is not just another STM program. While there are, of course, parallels, and there are common challenges and obstacles between EdSTM and other STM programs, there are distinct differences, as well, and EdSTM stands up well under the criticisms leveled against STM, generally. For instance, a common objection to STMs, in general, is that such short visits do not allow the missionary to gain a proper grasp of the target culture. However, that objection is far more defensible against the typical STM trip where Westerners are attempting to introduce Christ into a foreign culture to a stranger with no conception of the underpinnings of Christianity, which the missionary presupposes. To this can be added the language barriers, the time restraints (because so much time must be devoted to whatever the missions project is defined to be), and the general lack of biblical knowledge (or at least preparation) on the part of the STMer. Conversely, in the model proposed herein, the student is a pastor (or a group of pastors) who, by definition, already accepts the foundational premises of the missionaries' message – and is in fact eager to receive that message. Also, in this model, the teacher is prepared, having been trained himself and possessing resource materials in both his language and that of the receptor culture.[9]

Further, in most parts of the world, there is at least occasional access to the Internet; thus EdSTM can encourage the EdSTMer and the indigenous pastor(s) with whom he worked to stay in touch after the missions trip, develop a relationship built

9. Of course, the necessity of an interpreter remains an issue in this model, as it does in most STMs.

upon their time spent together studying God's Word, and engage in genuine discipleship. Where the Internet is not available, there are more antiquated means of communication that could be employed. As suggested above, EdSTMers may well choose to study a different subject and then return to the same region and further develop this relationship. While traditional STM models may *allow* for the nurturing of such relationships, the *actualization* of such relationships is rare in that context, as the vision of most STM activities is more likely to be focused on the immediate (evangelism for conversions, relief efforts, building projects, etc.) and less likely to be focused on such long-rage goals as spiritual maturity and ministerial replication.

There are additional benefits to this model, both for the receptor culture and the West. First, as with all STM trips, it allows the receptor culture to understand that they are part of the global church. This is particularly significant in an isolated nation and, in concert with the nurturing and discipleship described above, could serve to foster an attitude of true *koinonia* and displace the fears and insecurities that plague many local believers. Second, this model—unlike typical STMs—allows for the pastors to receive fresh biblical insights as well as being introduced to new delivery methodologies as they interact with both the EdSTMer and the resource material.

There are also benefits for the EdSTMer and his home church. First, as with all STMs, this model serves to increase awareness of the receptor culture. In the case of a nation that is virtually unknown to many Americans, this opens the door to reciprocal prayer and Christian fellowship, vicariously, through the personal and growing bond between the indigenous pastor and the EdSTMer. Finally, unlike most STM trips, this model engages those in the local, American church who have teaching gifts and hearts for missions, and yet it does so without demanding of them a commitment to full-time vocational missions. In the end, the local church, the indigenous church, and, in fact, the global church, is edified and encouraged, as the people of God grow closer to one another and, in the process, closer to the One for whom they are named.

Glossary

Missions. The term "missions," as used in this book, refers to that collective work of the evangelical church to expose the world to the gospel of Christ and make disciples of those who are converted, as instituted by Christ in the Great Commission (Matt 28:19–20). This would include, generally, any efforts to reach this objective, such as church planting, relational evangelism and tentmaking strategies,[1] translation (of Bible and/or secondary material), as well as relief and development.[2]

Educational Missions. "Educational missions," for the purposes of this book, refers specifically to the objective of providing biblical and/or theological education in an indigenous, missions context. This would, therefore, exclude the common missions vehicles of, for instance, teaching English or vocational skills.

Short-Term Missions (STM). "Short-term missions" is a term variously defined as involving less than two weeks,[3] any time less than one year,[4] or even as long as two years.[5] For the purposes of this book—and this model—STM is defined as less than two weeks.

    1. "Tentmaking" refers to finding employment as a means to become embedded in a foreign culture, while engaging in missions ministry around that employment.
    2. Provided such work is engaged with the ultimate objective of conveying the gospel and/or training or discipling the indigenous church.
    3. Weber, *Missions Handbook*, 238.
    4. Slater, "Short-Term Missions," 452.
    5. Moreau, *Introducing World Missions*, 254.

Glossary

Those involved in such missions, or, short-term missionaries, are identified as STMers.

Educational Short-Term Missions (EdSTM). This term refers to STMs focused on providing theological education to indigenous pastors. In the context of this book, these would be *non-professional ministers* (see below). Those engaged in this work are identified as EdSTMers.

Majority World. The evangelical missions community has variously employed a number of terms to indicate what has historically and politically been referred to as the Third World. Among these terms are *Global South, underdeveloped world, developing world,* and *World A*.[6] The term, *Majority World*, has become increasingly popular and is used in this book to refer to those nations and people groups most in need of EdSTM; namely, those with extremely low to low economic resources, and with little to no access to formal theological training.

Nonprofessional Missionaries. This term is employed to refer to any persons who engage in STM who are neither vocational missionaries nor ministers. Thus, the pastor who is also a STMer would *not* be a nonprofessional missionary.[7]

---

6. Ibid., 13.

7. This term was first introduced by Roland Allen ("Non-Professional Missionaries," 195-201).

Appendix A

Church Survey Questions and Results

1. Does your church support Long Term Missionaries (LTMs) and, if so, how many does your church support?[1]

	Respondents	Percentage
1	2	2.2
2	19	21.8
3	24	27.6
4	11	12.6
5 or more	24	27.6

2. How many of the LTMs you support are principally focused on the following:

	Respondents	Percentage
Evangelism	42	48.2
Church Planting	14	16.1
Relief efforts/Social Aid	0	n/a
Discipleship Training of Indigenous Pastors	23	26.4
Other	8	9.1

1. Eighty-seven churches were surveyed. Not all results total 100 per cent due to rounding and unanswered questions on some surveys.

Appendix A: Church Survey Questions and Results

3. How many Short Term Mission (STM) trips does your church typically organize each year?

	Respondents	Percentage
None	15	17.2
1-3	44	50.1
4-6	15	17.2
More than 6	10	11.5

4. Of these, how many are typically "team" trips, involving 4 or more participants?

	Respondents	Percentage
<25%	6	6.9
26%-50&	32	36.8
51%-75%	21	24.1
76%-100%	26	29.9

5. What is the primary nature of the STM trip(s)?

	Respondents	Percentage
Social/Economic Development (building projects [e.g. wells, schools, churches], rehabilitation programs)	27	31.0
Humanitarian Aid (e.g., disaster relief, crisis intervention)	11	12.6
Relational Evangelism (i.e., evangelism in the context of other activities, such as social/economic development projects or humanitarian aid)	21	24.1

Appendix A: Church Survey Questions and Results

	Respondents	Percentage
Intentional Evangelism (e.g., street witnessing)	11	12.6
Educational/Discipleship Training (e.g., directing focused biblical/theological studies)	12	13.8
TESL (Teaching English as a Second Language)	2	2.3
Other	3	3.4

6. Does your church offer Adult Sunday School or Discipleship Classes?

	Respondents	Percentage
Yes	75	86.2
No	8	9.2

7. If 'yes,' have any of the teachers of these classes ever been involved in teaching in a foreign missions context?

	Respondents	Percentage
Yes	40	46.0
No	10	11.4
Unsure	32	36.8

8. Church Size (Classification Data)

	Respondents	Percentage
<100	17	19.5
101-250	29	33.3
251-500	18	20.7

Appendix A: Church Survey Questions and Results

	Respondents	Percentage
501-1000	8	9.2
1001-2500	9	10.3
>2500	6	6.9

9. Church Setting (Classification Data):

	Respondents	Percentage
Urban	22	25.3
Suburban	50	57.4
Rural	15	17.2

10. Which of the following best describes your church?

	Respondents	Percentage
Assemblies of God	3	3.4
Baptist	36	41.4
Lutheran	2	2.3
Methodist	3	3.4
Non-denominational	23	26.4
Pentecostal	6	6.9
Presbyterian	6	6.9
Reformed	1	1.1
Other	7	8.0

Appendix B

Missions Agency Survey Questions and Results

1. Does your organization send:

	Respondents	Percentage
Long-term missionaries	0	n/a
Short-term missionaries	0	n/a
Both	21	100

2. What is your organization's primary work? (choose the one answer that best describes your focus)

	Respondents	Percentage
Evangelism	2	9.5
Biblical Translation	1	4.7
Bible Distribution	0	n/a
Humanitarian Aid, Crisis Intervention	3	14.3
Social/Economic Development Projects	2	9.5
Church Planting	11	52.4
Educational/Discipleship Training (not including TESL)	2	9.5
TESL (Teaching English as a Second Language)	0	n/a

Appendix B: Missions Agency Survey Questions and Results

3. What area/region best describes your organization's target field?

	Respondents	Percentage
Africa	4	19
Asia	2	9.5
Europe, Eastern	1	4.8
Europe, Western	1	4.8
Latin America	2	9.5
North America	1	4.8
"10/40 Window" Nations	1	4.8
Muslim World	3	14.2
Global	6	28.5

4. If your organization engages short-term missionaries, what best describes their area of involvement?[1]

	Respondents	Percentage
Evangelism	2	9.5
Biblical Translation	0	n/a
Bible Distribution	0	n/a
Humanitarian Aid, Crisis Intervention	5	23.8
Social/Economic Development Projects	9	42.9
Church Planting	1	4.8
Educational/Discipleship Training (not including TESL)	4	19.0
TESL (Teaching English as a Second Language)	0	n/a

1. Cumulative totals may exceed 100%, as respondents were allowed to select more than one response.

Appendix B: Missions Agency Survey Questions and Results

5. If your organization engages short-term missionaries, are they[1]:

	All		Most (>50%)		Some (<50%)		None	
	#	%	#	%	#	%	#	%
Vocational (ordained) ministers– actively serving (e.g., pastors)	0	n/a	4	19.0%	9	42.8%	0	n/a
Ordained but retired (or otherwise inactive) ministers	0	n/a	2	9.5%	6	28.6%	0	n/a
Laypersons	0	n/a	15	71.4%	12	57.1%	0	n/a

Appendix C

Pastor's Interview Questions and Responses

Pastor #1 (Burma)

1. How long have you been involved in ministry?[1]

   14 years

2. Have you ever had occasion to work in your country with missionaries from the West?

   Yes

   a. If so, what is/was the nature of the missionaries' work while in your country?

   Teaching us doctrine (this author)

   b. If not, are you familiar with any Western missionaries who have worked in your country (with someone other than yourself)? If so, what is/was the nature of their work?

   c. Have you ever sought to have missionaries work with you in your country?

   No

---

1. The responses in the following series reflect the content, if not the participants' verbatim dialogue, as the interviews were conducted via a series of communications (personal conversation and/or email) and occasionally through interpreters.

Appendix C: Pastor's Interview Questions and Responses

3. Regarding theological education in your country:

    a. Is there presently access to evangelical Bible schools/seminaries?

    Yes

    i. If so, is that access cost-prohibitive or otherwise impractical, in your opinion?

    Not a real option; the cost is very much and the school is dedicated to a different tribe

    ii. If not, do your pastors have any other access to formal theological instruction? Explain.

    We have some books that we use and some notes from a pastor who attended Bible college

4. Regarding Western missionaries working as theological instructors in your country:

    a. Do you think such ministry is needed?

    Yes

    b. Would you be willing to serve as liaison between such ministry and pastors in your area?

    Yes, I already do that (with this author)

Pastor #2 (Philippines)

1. How long have you been involved in ministry?

    8 years

2. Have you ever had occasion to work in your country with missionaries from the West?

    Yes

Appendix C: Pastor's Interview Questions and Responses

- a. If so, what is/was the nature of the missionaries' work while in your country?

    (This author) holding classes

- b. If not, are you familiar with any Western missionaries who have worked in your country (with someone other than yourself)? If so, what is/was the nature of their work?

- c. Have you ever sought to have missionaries work with you in your country?

    We asked some on the Internet, but none came (except this author)

3. Regarding theological education in your country:

    a. Is there presently access to evangelical Bible schools/seminaries?

    Yes

    - i. If so, is that access cost-prohibitive or otherwise impractical, in your opinion?

        They are all very far away from village

    - ii. If not, do your pastors have any other access to formal theological instruction? Explain.

        My father went to Bible college for a year and he teaches some of the pastors here

4. Regarding Western missionaries working as theological instructors in your country:

    a. Do you think such ministry is needed?

    Yes

    b. Would you be willing to serve as liaison between such ministry and pastors in your area?

    Yes

Appendix C: Pastor's Interview Questions and Responses

Pastor #3 (Philippines)

1. How long have you been involved in ministry?

   32 years

2. Have you ever had occasion to work in your country with missionaries from the West?

   Yes

   a. If so, what is/was the nature of the missionaries' work while in your country?

   Evangelistic crusades; teaching (this author), emergency relief

   b. If not, are you familiar with any Western missionaries who have worked in your country (with someone other than yourself)? If so, what is/was the nature of their work?

   c. Have you ever sought to have missionaries work with you in your country?

   Yes

3. Regarding theological education in your country:

   a. Is there presently access to evangelical Bible schools/seminaries?

   Yes

   i. If so, is that access cost-prohibitive or otherwise impractical, in your opinion?

   Costs are high, plus distance is a problem for our people

   ii. If not, do your pastors have any other access to formal theological instruction? Explain.

   There really is no option for our pastors at this time, except when teachers come (this author)

Appendix C: Pastor's Interview Questions and Responses

4. Regarding Western missionaries working as theological instructors in your country:

   a. Do you think such ministry is needed?

   Yes

   b. Would you be willing to serve as liaison between such ministry and pastors in your area?

   Yes

Pastor #4 (Burma)

1. How long have you been involved in ministry?

   12 years

2. Have you ever had occasion to work in your country with missionaries from the West?

   Yes

   a. If so, what is/was the nature of the missionaries' work while in your country?

   Varied; a lot of humanitarian work, some evangelism and church planting

   b. If not, are you familiar with any Western missionaries who have worked in your country (with someone other than yourself)? If so, what is/was the nature of their work?

   c. Have you ever sought to have missionaries work with you in your country?

   Yes

3. Regarding theological education in your country:

Appendix C: Pastor's Interview Questions and Responses

    a. Is there presently access to evangelical Bible schools/seminaries?

    Yes

        i. If so, is that access cost-prohibitive or otherwise impractical, in your opinion?

        We have a seminary that is accessible to us; the cost is an issue, but we can sometimes get scholarships

        ii. If not, do your pastors have any other access to formal theological instruction? Explain.

4. Regarding Western missionaries working as theological instructors in your country:

    a. Do you think such ministry is needed?

    Any teaching of the Bible would be welcome

    b. Would you be willing to serve as liaison between such ministry and pastors in your area?

    If possible

Pastor #5 (Uganda)

1. How long have you been involved in ministry?

    21 years

2. Have you ever had occasion to work in your country with missionaries from the West?

    Yes

    a. If so, what is/was the nature of the missionaries' work while in your country?

    Bible translation, evangelism, teaching (this author), humanitarian work

Appendix C: Pastor's Interview Questions and Responses

    b. If not, are you familiar with any Western missionaries who have worked in your country (with someone other than yourself)? If so, what is/was the nature of their work?

    c. Have you ever sought to have missionaries work with you in your country?

I have not played a role in personally inviting missionaries, but I have welcomed them

3. Regarding theological education in your country:

    a. Is there presently access to evangelical Bible schools/seminaries?

Yes

        i. If so, is that access cost-prohibitive or otherwise impractical, in your opinion?

Only the wealthiest can attend such schools

        ii. If not, do your pastors have any other access to formal theological instruction? Explain.

A few of our pastors have had the opportunity to study courses, and teaching missionaries (this author and others)

4. Regarding Western missionaries working as theological instructors in your country:

    a. Do you think such ministry is needed?

Definitely

    b. Would you be willing to serve as liaison between such ministry and pastors in your area?

If asked, of course

Appendix C: Pastor's Interview Questions and Responses

Pastor #6 (Nepal)

1. How long have you been involved in ministry?

   13 years

2. Have you ever had occasion to work in your country with missionaries from the West?

   Yes

   a. If so, what is/was the nature of the missionaries' work while in your country?

      Evangelism, humanitarian work

   b. If not, are you familiar with any Western missionaries who have worked in your country (with someone other than yourself)? If so, what is/was the nature of their work?

   c. Have you ever sought to have missionaries work with you in your country?

   Yes

3. Regarding theological education in your country:

   a. Is there presently access to evangelical Bible schools/seminaries?

      No

      i. If so, is that access cost-prohibitive or otherwise impractical, in your opinion?

      ii. If not, do your pastors have any other access to formal theological instruction? Explain.

      We teach one another as we are able; two of our pastors were able to attend seminary briefly, and when they are in the region, they offer Bible studies

Appendix C: Pastor's Interview Questions and Responses

4. Regarding Western missionaries working as theological instructors in your country:

    a. Do you think such ministry is needed?

    Most definitely

    b. Would you be willing to serve as liaison between such ministry and pastors in your area?

    Yes

Pastor #7 (Nepal)

1. How long have you been involved in ministry?

    6 years

2. Have you ever had occasion to work in your country with missionaries from the West?

    No

    a. If so, what is/was the nature of the missionaries' work while in your country?

    b. If not, are you familiar with any Western missionaries who have worked in your country (with someone other than yourself)? If so, what is/was the nature of their work?

    I know that missionaries serve in my country feeding the hungry

    c. Have you ever sought to have missionaries work with you in your country?

    No

Appendix C: Pastor's Interview Questions and Responses

Regarding theological education in your country:

d. Is there presently access to evangelical Bible schools/seminaries?

No

    i. If so, is that access cost-prohibitive or otherwise impractical, in your opinion?

    ii. If not, do your pastors have any other access to formal theological instruction? Explain.

    Only what we are able to do ourselves, or when foreigners come

3. Regarding Western missionaries working as theological instructors in your country:

    a. Do you think such ministry is needed?

    Yes

    b. Would you be willing to serve as liaison between such ministry and pastors in your area?

    Yes

Pastor # 8 (Ghana)

1. How long have you been involved in ministry?

    26 years

2. Have you ever had occasion to work in your country with missionaries from the West?

    Yes

    a. If so, what is/was the nature of the missionaries' work while in your country?

    Evangelism, discipleship, church planting, disaster relief

Appendix C: Pastor's Interview Questions and Responses

    b. If not, are you familiar with any Western missionaries who have worked in your country (with someone other than yourself)? If so, what is/was the nature of their work?

    c. Have you ever sought to have missionaries work with you in your country?

    Yes

3. Regarding theological education in your country:

    a. Is there presently access to evangelical Bible schools/seminaries?

    Yes

        i. If so, is that access cost-prohibitive or otherwise impractical, in your opinion?

        It is expensive, but those who are called to be pastors can usually go to school

        ii. If not, do your pastors have any other access to formal theological instruction? Explain.

4. Regarding Western missionaries working as theological instructors in your country:

    a. Do you think such ministry is needed?

    Every opportunity to learn is positive

    b. Would you be willing to serve as liaison between such ministry and pastors in your area?

    My schedule is very full, but I would if it were needed and no one else would

Appendix C: Pastor's Interview Questions and Responses

Pastor # 9 (Uganda)

1. How long have you been involved in ministry?

   10 years

2. Have you ever had occasion to work in your country with missionaries from the West?

   Yes

   a. If so, what is/was the nature of the missionaries' work while in your country?

   Evangelism, apologetic debates, humanitarian work, teaching (not this author)

   b. If not, are you familiar with any Western missionaries who have worked in your country (with someone other than yourself)? If so, what is/was the nature of their work?

   c. Have you ever sought to have missionaries work with you in your country?

   No

3. Regarding theological education in your country:

   a. Is there presently access to evangelical Bible schools/seminaries?

   Only on the other side of the county

   i. If so, is that access cost-prohibitive or otherwise impractical, in your opinion?

   The schools are several hours drive away and very expensive also

   ii. If not, do your pastors have any other access to formal theological instruction? Explain.

   Some pastors here hold classes and missionaries teach (this author and others)

Appendix C: Pastor's Interview Questions and Responses

4. Regarding Western missionaries working as theological instructors in your country:

    a. Do you think such ministry is needed?

    Yes

    b. Would you be willing to serve as liaison between such ministry and pastors in your area?

    Yes

Pastor # 10 (Philippines)

1. How long have you been involved in ministry?

    8 years

2. Have you ever had occasion to work in your country with missionaries from the West?

    Yes

    a. If so, what is/was the nature of the missionaries' work while in your country?

    Bible translation, humanitarian work, teaching (this author)

    b. If not, are you familiar with any Western missionaries who have worked in your country (with someone other than yourself)? If so, what is/was the nature of their work?

    c. Have you ever sought to have missionaries work with you in your country?

    No

Appendix C: Pastor's Interview Questions and Responses

3. Regarding theological education in your country:

    a. Is there presently access to evangelical Bible schools/seminaries?

    Yes

    i. If so, is that access cost-prohibitive or otherwise impractical, in your opinion?

    It is very expensive; I am the only pastor from our region who has been

    ii. If not, do your pastors have any other access to formal theological instruction? Explain.

    I teach the other pastors when I have the opportunity

4. Regarding Western missionaries working as theological instructors in your country:

    a. Do you think such ministry is needed?

    Yes

    b. Would you be willing to serve as liaison between such ministry and pastors in your area?

    Yes

Bibliography

Allen, Roland. "Non-Professional Missionaries." In *Missionary Principles*, edited by Roland Allen. London: World Dominion, 1964.

Anderson, Courtney. *To the Golden Shore: The Life of Adoniram Judson*. Boston: Little Brown, 1956.

Anthony, Michael J., ed. *The Short-Term Missions Boom*. Grand Rapids: Baker, 1994.

Bahamonde, Marcos Arroyo. "Contextualization of Mission: A Missiological Analysis of Short-Term Missions." *The Journal of Latin American Theology* 2 (2007) 227–48.

Beuttler, Fred W. "Evangelical Missions in Modern America." In *The Great Commission: Evangelicals and the History of World Missions*, edited by Martin I. Klauber and Scott M. Manetsch, 108–32. Nashville: Broadman and Holman, 2008.

Blue, J. Ronald. "The Necessity of Theological Training for the Missionary." In *Overcoming the World Missions Crisis*, edited by Russell L. Penney, 173–88. Grand Rapids: Kregel, 2001.

———. "Tell the Story." In *Stepping Out—A Guide to Short-Term Missions*, edited by Steve Hawthorne, 179–82. Monrovia, CA: Short-Term Missions Advocates, 1987.

Carson, D. A. "Ongoing Imperative for World Mission." In *The Great Commission*, edited by Martin I. Klauber and Scott M. Manetsch, 176–95. Nashville: B & H, 2008.

Clark, Michael P. ed. *The Eliot Tracts*. Westport, CT: Praeger, 2003.

Collins, Jennifer. "Short-Term Missions." In *Overcoming the World Missions Crisis*, edited by Russell L. Penney, 304–41. Grand Rapids: Kregel, 2001.

Cook, Charles A. "Assessing the Long-Term Impact of Intercultural Sojourns: Contributions of Canadian Bible College Intercultural Sojourns in Developing Global Awareness." PhD diss., Trinity International University, 2005.

Cook, Charles A., and Joel Van Hoogan. "Towards a Missiologically and Morally Responsible Short-Term Ministry: Lessons Learned in the Development

Bibliography

of Church Partnership Evangelism." *Journal of Latin American Theology* 2 (2007) 48–68.

Cooke, Robert. "Good News, Bad News: North American Protestant Overseas Personnel Statistics in Twenty-Five Year Perspective." *International Bulletin of Mission Research* 19 (January 1995) 6–8, 10–13.

Cooney, Michael. "US Snapshot of Broadband World Finds Disparity and Dial-Up." http://www.networkworld.com/community/blog/us-snapshot-broadband-world-finds-disparity-a.

Creson, Bob. "Global Perspective." In *Global Mission Handbook: A Guide for Crosscultural Service*, edited by Steve Hoke and Bill Taylor, 188–9. Downers Grove: IVP, 2009.

Curtis, Steve. "In Prayer and Pains, through Faith in Christ: The Life and Ministry of John Eliot." *Missiology: An International Review* 43 (2015) 137–47.

Elmer, Duane. *Cross-Cultural Connections*. Downers Grove: IVP, 2002.

Ethnologue. http://www.ethnologue.com.

Fanning, Don. "Short-Term Missions: A Trend that is Growing Exponentially." http://tinyurl.com/ajb7mhn.

Fernando, Ajith. "Getting Back on Course." *Christianity Today*, November 2007.

Finke, Roger. *The Churching of America, 1776–2005: Winners and Losers in Our Religious Economy*. Rutgers University Press, 2005.

Fischer, John. *Fearless Faith*. Eugene, OR: Harvest House, 2002.

Frame, John M. "Learning at Jesus' Feet: A Case for Seminary Training." http://www.frame-poythress.org/learning-at-jesus-feet-a-case-for-seminary-training/.

Frame, Randy. "Is Seminary Education Always Necessary for Pastoral Ministry?" http://seminarygradschool.com/article/Is-Seminary-Education-Always-Necessary-for-Pastoral-Ministry%3F.

Franciscan Experience, The. *St. Francis and St. Clare— life and times*. http://www.christusrex.org/www1/ofm/fra/FRAlife5.html.

Glasser, Arthur F., and Donald A. McGavran. *Contemporary Theologies of Mission*. Grand Rapids: Baker, 1985.

González, Justo. *The Story of Christianity, vol. 1: The Early Church to the Dawn of the Reformation*. New York: HarperOne, 1984.

Guthrie, Stan. *Missions in the Third Millennium: 21 Key Trends for the 21st Century*. Carlisle: Paternoster, 2000.

Hickson, Jon N. "Missions among Puritans and Pietists." In *The Great Commission: Evangelicals and the History of World Missions*, edited by Martin I. Klauber and Scott M. Manetsch, 23–43. Nashville: Broadman and Holman, 2008.

Hoke, Steve, and Bill Taylor. "Hands-On Missionary Training." In *Global Mission Handbook: A Guide for Crosscultural Service*, edited by Steve Hoke and Bill Taylor. 208–11. Downers Grove: IVP, 2009.

Howell, Brian. "Mission to Nowhere: Putting Short-Term Mission in Context." *International Bulletin of Missionary Research* 33 (October 2009) 206–11.

Bibliography

Hughes, Philip, ed. and trans., *The Register of the Company of Pastors of Geneva in the Time of Calvin*. Grand Rapids: Wm. B. Eerdmans, 1966.
Index Mundi. http://www.indexmundi.com/g/r.aspx?t=0&v=67&l=en.
Internet World Statistics. http://www.internetworldstats.com/stats.htm.
Jaffarian, Michael. "Good News and Bad News in the North American Missions Movement." In *Global Mission Handbook*, edited by Steve Hoke and Bill Taylor, 178-9. Downers Grove: IVP, 2009.
———. "The Statistical State of the North American Protestant Missions Movement, from the Mission Handbook, 20th edition." *International Bulletin of Missionary Research* 32 (January 2008) 35-38.
James, III, Frank A. "Calvin and Missions." *Christian History* 5:4 (Fall 1986) 23-24.
James, R. Alton. "Post-Refomation Missions Pioneers." In *Discovering the Mission of God: Best Missional Practices for the 21st Century*, edited by Mike Barnett, 250-66. Downers Grove: IVP, 2012.
Joshua Project. http://www.joshuaproject.net.
Kaiser, Walter C. "Israel's Missionary Call." In *Perspectives on the World Christian Movement*, 3rd ed., edited by Ralph D. Winters and Steven C. Hawthorne, 10-16. Pasadena: William Carey Library, 2009.
Kane, J. Herbert. *Life and Work on the Mission Field*. Grand Rapids: Baker, 1980.
———. *Understanding Christian Missions*. Grand Rapids: Baker, 1986.
Kee, Howard Clark, et al. *Christianity: A Social and Cultural History*. New York: Macmillan, 1991.
Kinsler, F. Ross. *The Extension Movement in Theological Education*. Pasadena: William Carey International University Press, 1978.
Koch, Bruce A. "The Surging Non-Western Mission Force." In *Perspectives on the World Christian Movement*, 3rd ed., edited by Ralph D. Winters and Steven C. Hawthorne, 370. Pasadena: William Carey Library, 2009.
Koll, Karla Ann. "Taking Wolves among Lambs: Some Thoughts on Training for Short-Term Mission Facilitation." *International Bulletin of Missionary Research* 34 (April 2010) 93-96.
Kornfield, William J. "The Challenge to Make Extension Education Culturally Relevant." *Evangelical Missions Quarterly* 12 (January 1976) 13-22.
Latourette, Kenneth Scott. *The Great Century in Europe and the United States of America, A.D. 1800-A.D. 1914*, vol. 4 of *A History of the Expansion of Christianity*. NY: Harper and Brothers, 1944.
———. *The Great Century in Northern Africa and Asia, A.D. 1800-A.D. 1914*, vol. 6 of *A History of the Expansion of Christianity*. NY: Harper and Brothers, 1944.
Lupton, Robert. *Toxic Charity: How Churches and Charities Hurt Those They Help (and How to Reverse It)*. New York: HarperCollins, 2011.
Lyall, Leslie T. *A Passion for the Impossible: The Continuing Story of the Mission Hudson Taylor Began*. London: OMF Books, 1965.

Bibliography

Marsden, George M. *The Soul of the American University: From Protestant Establishment to Established Nonbelief.* Oxford, England: Oxford University Press, 1994.

Mather, Cotton. *Magnalia Christi Americana; or The Ecclesiastical History of New England.* 2nd ed. Edited by Thomas Robbins. Translated by Lucius F. Robinson, vol. 1. Hartford, CT: Silas Andrus and Son, 1855.

McManus, Erwin R. *An Unstoppable Force: Daring to Become the Church God Had in Mind.* Loveland, CO: Group, 2001.

Miley, George. "The Awesome Potential for Mission Found in Local Churches." In *Perspectives on the World Christian Movement*, 3rd ed., edited by Ralph D. Winters and Steven C. Hawthorne, 746–9. Pasadena: William Carey Library, 2009.

Miller, Glenn T. *Piety and Intellect: The Aims and Purposes of Ante-Bellum Theological Education.* Atlanta, GA: Scholars, 1990.

Moreau, A. Scott. Introduction to *Mission Handbook: U.S. and Canadian Protestant Ministries Overseas*, 21st ed., edited by Linda J. Weber. Wheaton: EMIS, 2010.

Moreau, A. Scott, et al. *Introducing World Missions: A Biblical, Historical, and Practical Survey.* Grand Rapids: Baker Academic, 2004.

Morton, Scott. *Funding Your Ministry: An In-Depth, Biblical Guide for Successfully Raising Personal Support.* Colorado Springs: NavPress, 2007.

Mulholland, Kenneth. "Missiological Education in the Bible College Tradition." In *Missiological Education for the Twenty-first Century: The Book, the Circle, and the Sandals: Essays in Honor of Paul E. Pierson*, 43–53. Eugene, OR: Wipf & Stock, 2005.

Nah, John S. "Rethinking Short-Term Missions Paradigms. Th.M. thesis, Fuller Theological Seminary, 2000.

Neill, Stephen. *A History of Christian Missions.* London: Penguin, 1990.

Norrish, Howard. "The Great Century." In *Discovering the Mission of God: Best Missional Practices for the 21st Century,* edited by Mike Barnett, 267–86. Downers Grove: IVP, 2012.

Olatoyan, Isaiah Oluwajemiriye. "The Local Church and the Great Commission: A Biblical Perspective on the Practice of Evangelism and Missions Among Churches of the Nigerian Baptist Convention." DMiss diss., Southern Baptist Theological Seminary, 2011.

Operation World. http://www.operationworld.org/; http://www.joshuaproject.net/.

People Groups. http://www.peoplegroups.org/.

Piper, John. *Let the Nations Be Glad! The Supremacy of God in Missions.* Grand Rapids: Baker, 1993.

Pirolo, Neal. "Raising the Standard for Missionary Care." In *Global Mission Handbook*, edited by Steve Hoke and Bill Taylor, 171–4. Downers Grove: IVP, 2009.

Pocock, Michael, et al. *The Changing Face of World Missions: Engaging Contemporary Issues and Trends.* Grand Rapids: Baker, 2005.

Bibliography

Priest, Robert J., and Joseph Paul Priest. "They See Everything, and Understand Nothing: Short-Term Mission and Service Learning." *Missiology: An International Review*, 36 (January 2008) 53–73.

Raines, Jeffrey. "An International Perspective on Short-Term Missions." D Min diss., Princeton Theological Seminary, 2008.

Sheets, Donna Leigh. "A Short-term Mission Trip Training Program with an Emphasis on Cross-Cultural Training and Reentry for Covenant Church in Winterville, North Carolina." DMin diss., Regent Divinity School, 2010.

Slater, Bryan A. "Short-Term Missions: Biblical Considerations." *Evangelical Missions Quarterly* 36 (October 2000) 452–7.

Stairs, Jonathan Edward. "A Global Approach for the Local Church as a Mission Agent and Agency." DMin diss., Liberty Baptist Theological Seminary, 2011.

Stanley, Paul, and J. Robert Clinton. *Connecting: The Mentoring Relationships You Need to Succeed in Life*. Colorado Springs: NavPress, 1992.

Stevens, Carly. "Recruitment and Training of Lay Missionaries." *Missio Apostolica* 17 (May 2009) 25–30.

Stott, John R. W. "The Living God is a Missionary God." In *Perspectives on the World Christian Movement*, 3rd ed., edited by Ralph D. Winters and Steven C. Hawthorne, 3–9. Pasadena: William Carey Library, 2009.

Strange, Alan D. "Seminary Education: Its Necessity and Importance." http://www.opc.org/new_horizons/NH99/NH9910a.html.

Sweeney, Douglas A. Introduction to *The Great Commission: Evangelicals and the History of World Missions*, edited by Martin I. Klauber and Scott M. Manetsch. Nashville: Broadman and Holman, 2008.

Tarantal, Peter. "Global Perspectives." In *Global Mission Handbook: A Guide for Crosscultural Service*, edited by Steve Hoke and Bill Taylor, 252–3. Downers Grove: IVP, 2009.

Taylor, Bill. "Flying with Two Wings: The Role of Short-Term Missions." In *Global Mission Handbook: A Guide for Crosscultural Service*, edited by Steve Hoke and Bill Taylor, 125–9 Downers Grove: IVP, 2009.

Tennent, Timothy C. *Invitation to World Missions: A Trinitarian Missiology for the Twenty-First Century*. Grand Rapids: Kregel, 2010.

———. "Top Ten Mission Trends in the Twenty-First Century: Pros and Cons of Short-Term Missions." http://timothytennent.com/2010/04/.

Tucker, Ruth A. *From Jerusalem to Irian Jaya*. Grand Rapids: Zondervan, 2004.

Van Engen, Charles E. "A Broadening Vision." In *Earthen Vessels: American Evangelicals and Foreign Missions, 1880-1980*, edited by Joel A. Carpenter and Wilbert R. Shenk, 202–32. Grand Rapids: Eerdmans, 1990.

Verkuyl, Johannes. "The Biblical Foundation for the Worldwide Missionary Mandate." In *Perspectives on the World Christian Movement*, 3rd ed., edited by Ralph D. Winters and Steven C. Hawthorne, 42–48. Pasadena: William Carey Library, 2009.

Weber, Linda J. ed., *Mission Handbook: U.S. and Canadian Protestant Ministries Overseas, 21st Edition*. Wheaton: EMIS, 2010.

Bibliography

Wendland, E.H. "Theological Education by Extension." http://www.wlsessays.net/bitstream/handle/123456789/675/WendlandTheological.pdf?sequence=1&isAllowed=y.

Widner, Wes. "Short-Term Missions Trips: Sanctified Vacations?" *Reason to Stand*. http://reasontostand.org/archives/2009/07/30/sanctified-vacations.

Winter, Ralph D. "The Greatest Danger: The Re-Amateurization of Missions." *Missions Frontiers Bulletin* (March–April 1996) 6.

———. *Theological Education by Extension*. Pasadena: William Carey International University Press, 2008.

———. "The Two Structures of God's Redemptive Mission." In *Perspectives on the World Christian Movement*, 3rd ed., edited by Ralph D. Winters and Steven C. Hawthorne, 244–53. Pasadena: William Carey Library, 2009.

World Christian Database. http://worldchristiandatabase.org/wcd/.

www.ingramcontent.com/pod-product-compliance
Lightning Source LLC
Chambersburg PA
CBHW071623170426
43195CB00038B/2044